Phantoms & Fairies

Phantoms & Fairies

tales of the supernatural in Angus and Dundee

Forbes Inglis

The Pinkfoot Press

Brechin, 2010

First published 2010 in Scotland by
The Pinkfoot Press
1 Pearse Street, Brechin, Angus DD9 6JR

Reprinted 2013

ISBN 9781874012603

Typeset and designed at The Pinkfoot Press
Printed by ScandinavianBook

Contents

Illustrations

Introduction

I decided to write this book after hearing the story of Desmond Arthur, the Montrose ghost. My investigations led me to understand that there were in fact a number of ghosts present at the former RAF base at Montrose and from that moment I was hooked on the paranormal.

Ghosts and other strange phenomena are in some ways like God in that many people, whether believers or not, have strong views on the subject.

For sites in rural locations I have given map references from the OS Landranger Maps, 1: 50,000 scale. To assist visitors where sites are open to the public I have included telephone numbers and website details rather than opening times as these are often subject to change. Visitors looking to investigate the locations should make contact to confirm opening hours and whether admission charges are levied.

Where sites are in private hands I would ask readers to respect the privacy of the owners and not intrude.

Finally, I hope that readers, whether they accept the existence of spirits or not, will enjoy finding out more about the places in Angus where there have been strange happenings and things apparently do go bump in the night!

Acknowledgements

My particular thanks for their assistance and cooperation to the Trustees and members of the Montrose Air Station Heritage Centre, Libby Reynolds and the staff at Glamis Castle, the Rev Margaret King, Elizabeth and Syd Walker, Dorothy Walker and Willy Newlands and to those named in individual stories, Laurie Rogers for the information on the Forfar spirits and the countless others who shared their experiences with me but did not wish to be identified and to all those who directed me towards a friend, relative or workmate "who had a story to tell".

Any errors or omissions are my own and I must take the blame for these.

Britain's Most Haunted Site?

The now disused Aerodrome at Montrose in the north east of Scotland has a long reputation of being haunted with various ghostly sightings of both planes and pilots having been reported over the years.

The story of the airfield began in the years just before the First World War when it became more and more obvious that the Germans were preparing for war.

During that period, Zeppelins, the giant German lighter than air machines, made regular excursions into what today we would call British air space with a view to spying on the British fleet. In the longer term it was possible that these airships would be used to attack British ships and bases.

With the Fleet based at Rosyth, near Edinburgh, and at Cromarty, in the north of Scotland, the then First Sea Lord, Winston Churchill, decided to protect these bases from the continuing aerial incursions by setting up the United Kingdom's first operational air station, midway between the two. The site chosen was at Upper Dysart Farm, some two miles south of Montrose on the A92.

The Royal Flying Corps (RFC), the forerunner of the Royal Air Force, was then stationed at Farnborough and, although no such exercise had ever been attempted before, the aircraft of No 2 Squadron were flown north, finally arriving at the new air station on 26th February 1913, having taken almost two weeks to complete the journey.

It had soon become obvious that the Upper Dysart field was unsuitable for flying and the Commanding Officer, Major C J Burke, searched the area for a more suitable site. He eventually decided that Broomfield Farm, just north of the town, offered a better situation and the decision was taken to transfer the air station there. Montrose Aerodrome opened in January 1914.

After World War I the airfield closed in 1920 but it was re-opened in 1935. From then until the end of World War II it served as a training base and, for a spell, it was also a base for operational flying.

There were many accidents and fatalities at Montrose and, as a result, it is believed to be one of the most haunted sites in the UK.

The Montrose Ghost

Mention the Montrose Ghost to anyone with knowledge of Scottish aviation or Montrose history and they will invariably know something about the fate of Desmond Arthur.

On Tuesday 29th April 1913, Lieutenant Desmond Lucius Arthur (**1**), a young Irishman, stepped off the train at Montrose Railway Station. Airmen had been coming and going from Montrose for several months by then and it is doubtful if anyone would have given the newcomer a second glance.

Yet the new man, who would never fire a shot in anger, was to become one of the most famous pilots in aviation history because of his violent death and its eerie aftermath.

Born on the 31st March 1884, Arthur had served with the 5th Royal Munster Hussars before obtaining his pilot's licence on 18th June 1912.

1 *Desmond Arthur: The Irishman was often described as 'fey' which can mean someone expected to die prematurely.*

2 *The wreckage of Arthur's aircraft at Lunan Bay.*

Just about one month after his arrival in Montrose, on 27th May 1913, while No 2 Squadron were still based at Upper Dysart, Arthur was killed when the biplane he was flying, a BE.2, broke up over Lunan Bay, just a few miles south of the town.

Arthur was thrown from the plane as it started to disintegrate and he fell some 2,000 feet to his death. Pilots were not given parachutes in those days.

According to an eye witness, the grieve (farm foreman) on Captain Blair-Imrie's farm, the accident happened just after 7.30 in the morning. He heard the plane going over but thought no more about it until he heard –

> a crashing noise. It wasn't the noise of an explosion, but more the sort of noise an axe makes when it's splitting wood, only much louder ...
>
> Suddenly I saw something black drop out of it. At first it didn't look any bigger than a ball, and I thought it was perhaps a bit that had broken off the machine. But before I'd time to wonder what it was I saw it was a man. He was coming down feet foremost, and his hands were held straight above his head. At first he didn't look to be dropping very fast, but by the time you would have counted to fifty he was full size ...
>
> He hit the earth and I started to run towards the spot, though I knew it wasn't a scrap of use (**2**).

Arthur's body was taken to Montrose Infirmary before being given a full military funeral (3) and interment at Sleepyhillock Cemetery on the outskirts of the town.

The Royal Aero Club, an independent body, investigated the crash and exonerated Arthur, concluding that a faulty repair to a wing spar had been the cause of the accident.

Aeroplane Disaster at Montrose.
Funeral of Lieut. Arthur.

3 *Arthur's funeral cortege makes its way into Montrose High Street.*

Despite the traumatic circumstances of Arthur's death, there was no immediate appearance by any ghostly figure seeking revenge or justice. For the time being at least, the spirit of Desmond Arthur appeared to be at peace.

A Reputation Questioned

It was only later, when another report was being prepared, this time blaming the unfortunate Arthur for his own death that the sightings started.

No one saw the ghost clearly enough to identify him and by the publication of the second report, most, if not all, of those who knew Arthur personally had been sent to France anyway.

It was the aviator and writer, C G Grey, himself a friend of Desmond Arthur, who first told the complete story in an article in The Aeroplane magazine in 1920 and suggested that the timing of the appearances meant that the spirit could be that of his late friend. Grey had the added advantage of knowing the individuals involved in the incidents although he refused to name them. His knowledge also meant that he was able to get accurate dates for the appearances

The alternative to the theory that the apparition was an innocent Desmond Arthur was that the ghost was that of an unhappy trainee, or 'hun' as the instructors called them, mainly because they reckoned the rookie pilots did more damage to the planes than the enemy ever managed. This particular hun had been sent up for a solo flight despite arguing that he did not feel like flying. He was killed and the belief was that he had returned to haunt the instructor whom he blamed for his death.

Grey argued, not unreasonably, that if every hun who was unhappy about flying and subsequently died came back to haunt his instructor the world would be awash with ghostly apparitions.

In 1916, the Government found themselves under attack from Pemberton Billings, an MP who was himself head of an aircraft company. Billing's argument was that the quality of aircraft then being manufactured was poor and had resulted in the unnecessary deaths of pilots.

The Government's response was to go on the attack and, in an attempt to both discredit Billings and bolster public confidence in the new flying machines, they set up their own committee to inquire into the death of Lt. Arthur. Although the truth was widely known throughout the RFC, this committee produced an Interim Report citing pilot error.

In the early days of the First World War, No 2 Squadron had left Montrose for France and probably few, if any, of the personnel at the Broomfield site, which was by then a training establishment, would have been Arthur's comrades. The officers at Montrose were still billeted in the old Militia Barracks however, as they had been from the setting up of the Dysart airfield.

In the autumn of 1916, just as the final Report was being prepared, there began a number of ghostly appearances at the Officers' Quarters, the one location still in use which would have been familiar to Arthur.

On several occasions, Major Cyril Foggin, one of the senior flying instructors, was walking towards the old Mess when he saw, in the darkness, a figure dressed in flying gear making its way to the door of the Mess. Once the figure reached the door however it vanished. Even in the dim light Foggin was certain that the apparition had not gone into the Mess or stepped off the path to either the right or left.

Initially, he put his visions down to overwork and tried to blot the episodes out of his mind.

Another officer awoke during the night with the feeling that there was someone else in the room. The coal fire gave sufficient light for him to make out a figure dressed in uniform sitting in the chair at the foot of his bed. He asked the apparition who he was and what he wanted but when he tried to get a closer look at his mysterious visitor the figure simply disappeared.

On another occasion, two officers sharing a room were both awakened by a similar feeling. One of them lit a match only to find that there was no one else in the room.

Eventually, as the story became more widely known, it became apparent that other officers had had similar experiences.

Some time before Christmas 1916, two members of the Inquiry team became aware of the original Aero Club investigation and, as a result of their findings, the Final Report was amended, clearing the unfortunate Arthur of any blame.

The ghost apparently made one last appearance in January 1917 when it was seen to throw some papers onto a fire in what may have been a final symbolic gesture; consigning the Interim Report to the flames perhaps?

Arthur – Fifty Years On

That was not the apparition's final appearance if the ghost story told by the well-known aviator, Sir Peter Masefield, about what happened to him in the early summer of 1963 is to be believed.

Sir Peter had flown north to Inverness in his Chipmunk to give a talk to a group of aviation enthusiasts. As often happens on these occasions, a number of people had gathered around the lounge fire in the hotel after the talk to have a few drinks and discuss 'old times'. Before

4 *Arthur's plane, a BE.2, before the crash*

long, someone brought up the topic of Montrose Aerodrome, Lt. Arthur and the infamous ghost.

After a member of the group had described Arthur's BE.2 as being brand-new, another speaker, sitting outside the firelight where he could not be seen, corrected this view. The mystery man, who spoke with an Irish accent, pointed out that the BE.2 had in fact been old and, having been fitted with a more powerful engine than it was originally designed to have, had been particularly difficult to fly.

Just as Sir Peter was preparing to leave Dalcross airfield the following morning, a figure in flying kit appeared and asked if he might have a lift to Farnborough or Brooklands. Sir Peter recognised the 'voice' from the previous evening and agreed.

The Chipmunk flew south using the east coast of Scotland as a navigational aid. As they crossed the river North Esk near Montrose, a BE.2 (**4**) of the type flown by Desmond Arthur emerged from a bank of cloud lying to the west. Sir Peter's Chipmunk, a more modern plane, was obviously much faster than the BE.2 and soon caught up with it until eventually the two planes were level about 200 feet apart.

Sir Peter could only watch in horror as the starboard wing of the BE.2 started to crumple and break up as the supporting struts fell away. The biplane continued to disintegrate until eventually the pilot was thrown from his seat into the air.

At that very moment Sir Peter heard a blood-curdling scream that caused him to turn round only to find that his companion had disappeared.

Somewhat shaken, he landed his plane on the old airfield and taxied over to some of the old buildings on the site where he spoke to some of the onlookers. No one had seen or heard anything other than his own plane and certainly no-one had seen any sign of a World War I biplane or anyone falling out of one.

On his return to the south Sir Peter completed his logbook entry of the events of the day. The date was 27th May 1963, exactly fifty years on from the date of the death of Lt. Desmond Arthur!

Although it is a good story that is all it is. Apart from some discrepancies in the local details there is also the fact that there was no connection between Arthur and Montrose Aerodrome. It quite simply didn't exist during his lifetime.

But did Lt. Desmond Arthur haunt the Officers' Quarters in an attempt to clear his name? Many people, then and now, believe that he did!

Arthur's Legacy

Today, the site of the old barracks is occupied by pharmaceutical giant Glaxo Smith Kline's factory car parks and warehouses but Desmond Arthur left another legacy as well as his ghostly attempts to clear his name.

In his will, he left the bulk of his estate to Winsome Constance Ropner, the daughter of a Hartlepool shipping magnate.

At the time of his death, Miss Ropner was almost 14 years old while Arthur was 29. Despite the age difference, Arthur apparently had a strong romantic attachment to the young woman and he carried a miniature portrait of her on his person at all times.

The Arthur family were unhappy about the contents of the will and the legacy was contested in the Irish courts. Desmond's brother, Charles, raised an action against Thomas Studdert and William Ropner, Winsome's father, who were the executors of the will.

The case came before Mr Justice Kenny at the Irish High Court in February 1914 and, like so much of Arthur's life and death, it raised more questions than answers.

Charles Augustus Arthur argued that the will, which was dated 17th July 1912, was not properly executed and that the testator, Desmond Arthur, did not know or approve of its contents.

The will left the bulk of the estate to Miss Ropner, with instructions to pay his brother the sum of £1,000, subject to her agreement.

During the hearing, the court heard of the attachment that the deceased obviously had to Miss Ropner and the story of the miniature was confirmed.

The will was holograph, i.e. written in the deceased's own handwriting, and had also been signed by two witnesses but, in yet another twist in the strange story of Desmond Arthur, neither of the witnesses could recall being asked to sign the document or remember anything about it.

Despite this testimony from the witnesses, Mr Justice Kenny decided to treat the case as if the witnesses to the will were dead and granted probate. Miss Ropner benefitted to the tune of something approaching £12,500.

Jinxed Flights?

To commemorate the 70th anniversary of Arthur's death 100 first day covers were produced to be sold to raise funds for the purchase of the old headquarters building for use as a museum to recognise the place of the air station at Montrose in RFC/RAF history.

As part of the campaign, it was decided that the covers would be flown around the airfield in a microlight and, on the 27th May 1983, Alistair Milne arrived at Broomfield, with his microlight, to prepare for the short flight.

For whatever reason, he was unable to get the engine started and the flight had to be abandoned amidst suggestions that perhaps the ghost had stopped the flight going ahead.

The following month, the first day covers successfully took to the air and were flown around the Broomfield airfield for approximately 11 minutes.

Worse was to follow however. Just under two years later, Alistair Milne, together with a passenger, Aileen Ross, the former wife of store magnate Sir Hugh Fraser, flew out over the North Sea and crashed into Inverbervie Bay. The bodies of Mr Milne and his passenger were recovered but the crashed aircraft was not, leaving experts to surmise the cause of the accident.

It had been suggested that the engine had been unreliable and this was thought to be the cause of the crash but there were those who believed that the connection with Arthur was more than just coincidence.

Between the Wars

With the War to end war over, there was no further need for so many airfields and the base at Montrose was closed in 1920 but, with further hostilities becoming increasingly likely, RAF Montrose was re-opened in the mid thirties.

Although the story of the 1916/17 hauntings was reputed to have spread throughout the Royal Flying Corps in France during the First World War there was no thought of ghostly activity when instructors, trainees and ground staff began to arrive at RAF Montrose in 1935.

If all seemed quiet it was not long however before tales of further ghostly sightings began to circulate.

The Ghostly Legends

One legend had suggested that the ghost would protect pilots and that there would be no further flying fatalities at Montrose until there was another war. This 'promise' seems to have been kept as, although flying training took place at the base, there were no deaths between 1936 and 1939. However, once the War started, fatal accidents began to occur regularly.

That said, one incident that had taken place earlier resurrected the idea that there was some sort of jinx affecting whole squadrons based at Montrose.

Away back in May 1914, the RFC decided to hold manoeuvres on Salisbury Plain and No 2 Squadron flew from their base at Montrose to take part. They had no problems until they reached Yorkshire where they found themselves enveloped in a thick fog. A number of planes crashed as a result of the weather conditions and pilot Lt. Empson and his mechanic George Cudmore were killed.

Although No 2 Squadron must have left Montrose later in 1914 to go to France there was no other movement involving a full squadron from Montrose until September 1933 when No 40 Bomber Squadron, having been based at Montrose while taking part in an exercise, flew south only to encounter similar problems in Northumberland where again two airmen died.

The coincidence was not lost on two former pilots who wrote jointly to Popular Flying magazine in April 1934 suggesting there could be 'some influence adverse to aviation associated with this old aerodrome'.

They advised that they did not believe in this 'spirit stunt, but it must be admitted that very strange things happen' and they remarked on the fact that on the last two occasions when complete squadrons had left Montrose they had encountered adverse weather conditions while other squadrons in the vicinity at the same time had experienced no problems.

> Upon attempting to return south No 40 Squadron RAF, following in the footsteps - or slipstream? – of No 2 Squadron RFC, experienced almost exactly the same form of disaster, yet other squadrons, who had not visited Montrose, and were returning at the same time as No 40, appear to have more or less got away with it. Certainly it is strange.

Another legend was that the Ghost would appear on a Wednesday and tap any pilot due to die the following day on the shoulder.

The basis of this story is probably because Desmond Arthur was believed to have died on a Thursday. In fact, the unfortunate Arthur was killed on a Tuesday and the mistake may have arisen because of delays in reporting the accident.

One pilot, said to have been tapped on the shoulder in this way, is reputed to have decided to avoid his fate by refusing to fly on the Thursday. He stayed in his billet, presumably having reported sick.

He was killed when a plane crashed on his hut! It is a fine spooky story but there is no evidence that such an incident ever happened.

In fact, an analysis of the accidents at the airfield over a period of some ten months revealed that fewer pilots died on Thursdays than on any other day of the week.

MONTROSE AERODROME A BUSY DAY

5 *Burke sheds (hangars) at RAF Montrose. WAAFS found the area particularly eerie and tried to avoid passing there at night.*

Footsteps

Not long after the base re-opened, Norrie Webster, an RAF policeman, was on a routine patrol in the early hours of the morning during either late autumn or early winter.

Mr Webster was walking southwards and he had just reached the stores when he heard footsteps coming towards him. Believing that it might be the orderly officer doing his early morning round he stopped and waited for him to appear.

The footsteps continued until they stopped, apparently right in front of Mr Webster, although he could see no one. The sound then moved off towards the workshops.

Mr Webster could give no logical explanation for what he had heard but he was determined to establish the source of the mysterious footsteps. As he followed he could hear the footsteps coming towards him again.

At that time there was a wooden projection attached to one of the sheds which was used for drying off the fire hoses after they had been used. The fire hoses would have been made of heavy canvas with brass nozzles on the end.

According to Mr Webster there was no wind at all that night, so he was surprised to see the hoses and their brass fittings swinging, as if moved by some unseen force.

Whatever Mr Webster may have thought afterwards about his strange experience he had it confirmed just a few days later. He was in the guardroom when the somewhat agitated members of the duty patrol burst in to announce that they had heard footsteps and seen a strange mist coming round the corner of the hangar used by A Flight.

The sound of the mysterious footsteps was heard in the area occupied by the former Indian Army sheds, later known as Burke sheds (**5**) after the first Commanding Officer, which had been used as hangars from the time of No2 Squadron. During WWII, few WAAFs would venture along past the old hangars at night, saying that the area was eerie and frightening.

A Loss of Evidence?

One of the earliest bombing raids on RAF Montrose occurred on 25th October 1940.

Three Heinkel IIIs appeared from the south and flew over the town, dropping bombs and strafing the High Street. When they reached the aerodrome they dropped more bombs, killing seven airmen and destroying a number of planes.

In addition, one of their bombs hit the Officers' Mess which was destroyed in the ensuing fire.

The Mess had housed the Station safe which contained the weekly wages for the serving personnel and a file, compiled by a Major Impey, on the subject of the Montrose Ghost.

The safe itself survived the fire and when it had cooled sufficiently to be opened the contents appeared to be intact. Once exposed to the air however the pound and ten shilling notes disintegrated, as did the file. No one will ever know what the file said and no copy has ever been found.

There have been suggestions however that the Major's report was 'excitable gibberish' and had been locked away so as not to cause panic.

The Roommate's Tale

6 *Brian C Robinson believed the ghost or ghosts saved his life on more than one occasion.*

On the 3rd October 1941 a young trainee pilot named George Hogben was killed when his plane crashed in the Angus Hills while on a solo training flight.

Hogben and his roommate, another trainee pilot called Brian C Robinson (**6**), were billeted in the area now occupied by Condor Crescent in Montrose.

Robinson must have been shocked that evening when Hogben, dressed in full flying kit, 'visited' him in their room.

George Hogben and Robinson were billeted in MQ 11 which was number 11 in a group of houses on the other side of the road that ran by the camp at Montrose.

I would imagine that the house and room probably still exist, albeit refurbished, in what is now called Condor Crescent.

On that particular day, Brian Robinson was in the room when the figure of Hogben appeared to him, dressed in flying kit, just as he would have been when he crashed.

He sat on his own bed, smiled and waved to Robinson, and then left through the window, as if it wasn't there.

Curiously enough, that is not the end of this particular story. I was present during a visit in the summer of 2005 to the former RAF Montrose Headquarters by paranormal investigators from the Scottish section of the Ghost Club, an organisation founded in 1862 which has included well-known names such as Charles Dickens and Sir Arthur Conan-Doyle, the creator of Sherlock Holmes, among its members.

One of the displays at the Montrose Air Station Heritage Centre, which is housed in the former Headquarters building, featured the Airfield

Ghosts but, other than the story of Desmond Arthur, all other material had been removed prior to the investigators arrival.

One of the investigating team, Joan Green, had been calling, without any apparent success, for any spirit present to make themselves known. I asked if she would like the name of someone who had served and died at RAF Montrose. Joan confirmed that she would accept a name so I gave her the name of George Hogben.

The call for any spirit to make contact was repeated, specifically using Hogben's name and as it was being made Lisa Bowell, a medium who is a member of the group, stated that she was feeling cold and 'getting' the name of Robinson, with a possible first name, Jack.

Coincidence? Perhaps, but of all the possible surnames it is a long shot that the name chosen was that of Hogben's roommate.

There is a popular saying, 'as quickly as you can say Jack Robinson', so I cannot even be certain that 'Jack' was not a nickname, like 'Dusty' Miller or 'Nobby' Clark.

Life Saving Ghosts

Mr Robinson himself believed that one of the ghosts – he had lost another friend in a training accident – saved his life on at least two occasions, otherwise he might have been another fatality.

On the first occasion, heavy fog, probably the sea haar which often drifts in with the tide, had covered the east coast but Mr Robinson believed that he survived thanks to the assistance of one of the airfield ghosts.

One bleak October day in 1941, Robinson had taken off from RAF Montrose, flying solo in a Master and, having completed his allotted exercise, he returned to base only to find that bad weather had come in obscuring the airfield.

It is hard to imagine a more worrying situation as Robinson had no radio contact with the ground, no radar and no radio-navigational aids.

Robinson himself found the events difficult to describe later but he swore that he had a vision that the ghost was with him and prevented him from crashing on a number of occasions.

Despite the conditions, he felt that he was guided to the only open spot in northeast Scotland that was clear of the all-embracing mist and fog and was able to land safely beside the River Bogie, some 60 miles from Montrose, with practically no fuel left in his tanks.

It is easy to dismiss Mr Robinson's story as nothing more than a piece of exceptional luck but RAF Montrose could be a dangerous place, particularly when there was little or no visibility. Sandwiched between the North Sea and the Angus Glens there was danger on either side for any pilot unfortunate enough to lose his bearings and a number of those killed while flying from Montrose either went down in the sea or crashed in the hills having lost their way.

The airfield was often the target for sneak hit-and-run raids by enemy bombers during the early part of the War and the second of Mr Robinson's narrow escapes came during one such incident.

Years later, Robinson clearly remembered this raid, convinced that his 'guardian' had been at his side that day.

He was walking towards a hut beside the airfield when he heard the drone of a twin-engined aircraft which he immediately recognised as that of a Heinkel IIIK. The German plane appeared to be coming straight towards him at low level and he could clearly see the air gunner in his turret, taking aim before opening up with his guns.

Caught out in the open, Robinson ran flat out for the nearest hut as a murderous hail of bullets ploughed into the ground all around him.

None of the enemy bullets struck him and he believed his escape from death on that occasion was a miracle which he could only attribute to the ghost

Describing the event later he wrote, 'There was certainly some super-natural force at work to save me that morning'.

There were other incidents involving other pilots in narrow escapes.

One such instance was a training flight involving two pupil pilots. They had left Montrose in fine conditions but during their flight the haar had again drifted in off the North Sea, obscuring both the airfield and the town.

Rather than risk crashing in the hills or in the sea, one of the pilots decided to try landing but in the atrocious weather conditions his plane crashed and he was killed instantly.

Strangely enough, the pilot of the second aircraft was able to find the airfield and land perfectly. Asked how he had managed, he replied that his dead friend had joined him in the cockpit and guided him in safely.

Phantom Planes

Squadron Leader Ovenden was based at RAF Montrose from March 1940 until October 1942.

One of the regular training routines involved trainee pilots taking off in darkness.

In order to achieve this, leading lights were set up about a mile upwind and to one side of the runway, presumably to provide the rookies with some guidance without putting the airfield itself in unnecessary danger. Normally, two airmen took the lights to the designated area in a van and then set them up.

In Squadron Leader Ovenden's own words:

> One night when I was aerodrome Control Pilot I found myself having my pre-sleep cup of tea at the end of the proceedings with two airmen who had been at a leading light set up, presumably near Rossie Castle.
>
> They asked me who had been killed in the crash. I told them there had been no crash.
>
> They were incredulous because both had seen the plane take off, catch fire and crash into the sand dunes. They were absolutely convinced.
>
> Nothing further transpired – I can vouch for these facts.

Subsequent embroidering of this story had the adjutant, Flying Officer Cribble, serving at Montrose in the First World War and remembering such a crash happening on the very same date in 1917/18.

Another Montrose Ghost?

Perhaps the above story can be linked to another bizarre happening at RAF Montrose.

It also involved a night flying exercise, this time in 1940. The pilots had to land by the light of a mobile beacon which was switched on just as a plane was heard and then off again as soon as the plane had landed safely.

On the night in question, the crew operating the beacon had counted eight aircraft out and back.

They were about to pack up when they heard the sound of another plane so they reactivated the beacon to allow the ninth aircraft to land. The 'extra' plane landed but blew up almost immediately.

Unable to account for the additional aircraft, telephone contacts were made to other RAF stations to see if any other base had a plane unaccounted for. The answer was no.

The most likely explanation seemed to be that an enemy aircraft had had to make a forced landing. In the circumstances there was nothing that could be done that night so it was decided that a full search of the airfield should be made the next morning.

When a line of servicemen, stretched right across the airfield, made a search the following morning no trace of a crashed aircraft could be found. Normally, some wreckage would be found but, although the crash had been witnessed by a large number of personnel, the plane had completely disappeared.

More Phantom Aircraft

These are not the only war time stories about phantom aircraft.

As well as being a training base RAF Montrose was also home to a detachment or flight of operational aircraft from the outbreak of War until 1943.

So when, during the early part of the War, a report was received to the effect that there was an enemy plane somewhere in the vicinity of the aerodrome a fighter was ordered into the air to seek out and destroy the intruder.

After about 30 minutes no contact had been made and the pilot was instructed to return to base.

Because of the danger of the airfield being attacked by enemy bombers the pilot had only a twin row of dim lights to guide him in to the landing strip.

Twice, the pilot, an experience flyer, made to touch down and on both occasions he aborted his landing at the final moment and roared off back into the night sky.

At that point it was decided to take a chance and light the runway more fully to allow the aircraft to land. This time there was no difficulty and the plane landed without any hitch.

It taxied in and stopped. As the pilot emerged from the cockpit it became obvious that he was angry and annoyed. "Who was the fool who cut me out?" he demanded to know.

"No one cut you out," someone replied.

"Of course someone did. Why do you think I went round again? Some madman in a biplane baulked me just as I was touching down – a thing like a Tiger Moth."

"There's no one else flying tonight," came the reply. "Besides, there isn't a biplane on the station."

The final phantom plane appeared sometime around Christmas during the 1980s. A lady, apparently a Mrs Carnegie, was driving her car down the part of the A92 from Arbroath to Montrose known locally as the Rossie Braes, when she saw what she later described as a khaki painted Second World War fighter. She could see the plane quite clearly and could even pick out the rivets on it but what struck her as particularly strange was that there was no engine noise.

She stopped her vehicle and got out but there was no sign of any plane and no noise.

The lady was convinced that she had seen a Spitfire or Hurricane and she contacted the local Museum to see if they could give her any explanation. Staff there put her in touch with officials at the Montrose Air Station Museum, now the Heritage Centre, who were able to confirm that they understood that at least two Hurricanes had crashed in the nearby Montrose Basin, the area of tidal water that lies to the west of the town.

Disappearing Pilots

As well as disappearing planes there have also been several instances of disappearing pilots at Montrose.

Jack Drummond, an aircraft fitter who was stationed at RAF Montrose from 1937 until War broke out, still lives in the town and tells of how one of his comrades saw the ghost.

The fire picket used a hut beside Waldron Bridge, the railway bridge that carried the main road into the camp and it was normal practice for each man on fire watch to be allowed half an hour to go to the canteen for a cuppa.

On one really nasty night of wind and rain, a man returned from his break remarking as he removed his sodden outwear, "I didn't think there would be any flying tonight."

The sergeant in charge was dismissive. "Course there won't be. Can't fly in this."

"Well," said the airman, "I passed someone dressed for flying on the bridge. He was wearing his helmet and goggles and a flying jacket. I spoke to him but he didn't say anything."

As he finished speaking it dawned on the other members of the fire picket that he might have seen the ghost. The sergeant took down the calendar that had been pinned on the wall. On the back was a newspaper cutting detailing the story of the hauntings.

The colour drained from the airman's face as he read through the cutting and realised that he had seen a ghost.

There is still no doubt in Jack's mind that the unfortunate airman believed that he had met the ghost

A similar story came from Mr M Stephenson, a ground gunner at RAF Montrose in 1942. When he went to relieve the lads who had been on night shift at the post just at the end of the railway bridge they told him they had seen a ghost. An airman, dressed in a white suit, had crossed the bridge and disappeared.

Certainly WWI airmen wore white overalls for flying so it may have been that what they had seen was a flashback to the time of the earlier conflict.

One theory, widely touted during the 1940s, was that the figure was an airman who had been shot as a WWI spy but the flyer had been innocent, hence his spirit's regular appearances to protest at the injustice of his sentence.

Whatever the apparition's motives, it would seem that the ghost on the bridge was a self-appointed guardian of his fellow pilots, often appearing in poor weather as if warning them not to fly.

He, assuming it is the same ghost, also appeared to a civilian worker called Hendry who had been asked to come and inspect an aircraft at the air station in 1942. As Mr Hendry was making his way home over Waldron Bridge he met a figure carrying a flying helmet.

It was a misty night and Mr Hendry remarked to the pilot that he was probably happy that there would be no flying that night.

The pilot didn't answer which Mr Hendry felt was odd. He looked back to discover that the figure had gone. Fearing that the pilot had fallen over the parapet of the bridge he searched the area but could find no trace of the mysterious flyer who seemed to have disappeared into thin air.

An Unwelcome Guest

Another tale of disappearing airmen was told to the late Ian McIntosh, the man behind the setting up of the Centre, by Alan Kettles, an Englishman who had been stationed at Montrose during World War II.

Ian and Alan were walking around the airfield in the company of Harry Jamieson when Alan pointed out the concrete base where the NAAFI building had been.

It was there, Alan told his small audience, that he came close to having an encounter with one of the many ghosts of Montrose airfield.

According to Alan, it was about 1500 hours on a working afternoon and he was standing on the airfield side of the NAAFI building watching the planes joining the circuit and preparing to land.

Suddenly, he heard a piercing scream coming from the NAAFI, followed by complete silence.

He and several others ran into the NAAFI to find one of the girls lying unconscious.

When she came round she explained what had happened.

She was in the habit of listening for the aircraft returning from training flights and when she heard the planes landing she would make the tea so that it was ready for the pilots when they came in.

That day, she had boiled up the urn and laid out tables for the returning pilots as normal. As she lifted the serving hatch she saw a pilot in full kit coming towards her but, just as she was about to hand him his mug of tea, he vanished!

What is also interesting about the story is that she apparently made no mention of the pilot being in any way strange, other than doing his disappearing act of course. Apart from the fact that the poor woman was undoubtedly suffering from shock, she would certainly have been familiar with the dress of WWII pilots so if the figure had been dressed in old fashioned RFC kit she would presumably have mentioned the fact.

It would appear therefore that 'her' ghost was from her own time.

The McIntosh family were involved in another ghost story.

Bill McIntosh, father of Ian and Graham who is still one of the driving forces behind the Centre, was a pilot himself during World War I and he always maintained that he had Goering in his sights but failed to shoot him down. Had he succeeded, he reckoned, he might just have changed the course of history.

During the Second War, Bill worked as a telephone linesman and was regularly called out, day and night, to RAF Montrose.

One particular night, the haar had rolled in off the sea creating, as it does, a sense of unreality and eeriness.

It has been suggested that the Montrose ghost was particularly active on these nights, although it is more likely that the haar simply helped create an atmosphere conducive to such fears.

One evening, with the weather as described, Bill, having repaired whatever fault he had been sent to deal with, was sitting in the guardroom having a well deserved cup of tea.

His relaxation was suddenly disturbed by the somewhat hysterical entrance of an airman who announced loudly that he had just seen the ghost.

The duty sergeant immediately took him to task for deserting his post as he was supposed to be guarding Waldron Bridge, the main route into the camp but, irrespective of the sergeant's ranting, the airman refused to go back.

Bill had no belief in ghosts so he volunteered to go out and see for himself. Drawing courage from the presence of another human being, and no doubt also fearful of the sergeant's wrath, the guard reluctantly agreed to show Bill the very spot where he had had his ghostly experience.

They made their way through the mist to the bridge where the airman pointed and announced he could still see the figure. Sure enough, there, barely discernible in the mist, was a ghostly outline.

Perhaps not so sure of himself as he had been, Bill approached the figure only to find as he got closer that it was a wooden signpost.

One can only imagine the ribbing the unfortunate airman must have received during the remainder of his time at RAF Montrose.

A Ghostly Conversation

When the War ended, unnecessary flying was stopped as quickly as possible in order to save fuel. With the development of the jet plane there was no place for RAF Montrose and its grass runways in the changing set up and the base was run down until its eventual closure in 1950.

Even after the War though, ghost activity continued to be reported.

Just a few years ago, I sat in the former headquarters building at Montrose aerodrome and listened to John Wears' story.

In September 1947, having just finished his basic training at RAF Innsworth, he was posted to RAF Montrose. Generally, newcomers soon found themselves on guard duty and the young Wears was no exception. That said, his experience was quite different from that of his fellows.

Most of them were probably unaware of Montrose's reputation for strange sightings but Wears didn't just see a ghost, he actually had a conversation with the apparition before it disappeared.

Wears was patrolling just opposite the Burke Sheds, the old 1914 hangars, in the area that the WAAFs avoided because of its eerie atmosphere.

Due to his youth and inexperience he admitted that he was nervous but he had been well drilled and his first stint, 1800 to 2000 hours, passed without incident.

His second spell of duty, between midnight and 0200, was more eventful however.

Not long after midnight he saw a strange glow moving along in front of the Burke sheds. It started to come towards him and he could hear the sound of footsteps. Eventually, he made out a shadowy figure which he proceeded to challenge.

In the time honoured manner he called out, "Halt, Who goes there," which initially met with no response, so he repeated the words.

It was only when he cocked his rifle and threatened, "Stop or I'll shoot," that the figure replied, "I am the Orderly Officer". Wears then called out, "Advance and be recognised".

As the figure emerged from the shadows the nervous young serviceman could see that the stranger had two rings on his uniform, similar to those worn by a flight lieutenant, but what was odd was that he was wearing a Sam Browne belt, not something that was RAF issue.

Faced with an officer, Wears sloped arms and gave him a butt salute which was returned in the conventional way before the 'Officer' asked, "Have you seen the patrol".

Telling the story in the Heritage Centre a few years ago, Wears pointed out that this was not an expression that was used in the RAF but he had been in the service for only a short time and he assumed that the officer meant the fire picket.

He looked away briefly to point out the direction that the fire picket had taken and when he turned back the figure had disappeared. A quick search of the immediate area failed to find any trace of his mysterious visitor.

At the end of his duty he reported as normal to his Duty Sergeant. When asked if he had anything to report he mentioned that he had met the Orderly Officer, a flight lieutenant.

The sergeant announced that the Orderly Officer on that particular night was a warrant officer and asked what the man looked like.

John described the uniform that the 'Officer' had been wearing and it was suddenly obvious to both of them that he was describing an RFC officer. (The RFC ceased to exist on 1st April 1918 when it became known as the Royal Air Force.)

Even then, it was years later before John Wears heard about Lieutenant Desmond Arthur and his apparent love of the airfield at Montrose but he felt that in this instance, ignorance was bliss.

The Flight Lieutenant's Return

Desmond Arthur was not the only spirit reputed to have returned to give a message to his former comrades.

One day in 1942, an extremely unpopular Flight Lieutenant, who had a fearsome reputation for flying off the handle about the least thing, had an argument with his fitter just before take off.

No one else was really sure whether the pilot was in the right or not but he had insisted on having the fitter put on a charge for his short-comings, whether real or imaginary.

The fitter himself was convinced that he was being picked upon unfairly and he resented the Flight Lieutenant's actions. He had support from other ground crew personnel, many of whom felt that the Officer had overreacted.

About a week later, the pilot took off again in a plane maintained by the same fitter. It subsequently crashed and the pilot was killed. An investigation took place but the cause of the crash could not be identified.

The rumour was that the fitter had taken his chance for revenge and made certain that the troublesome officer would not bother him or anyone else again.

Whether there was any truth in that allegation or not no one can tell but, soon after the crash, the figure of a ghostly pilot in flying kit began to make regular appearances on the airfield, as if attempting to unsettle the vengeful fitter.

Being on guard duty at the old base could seriously damage a serving airman's mental health. Many, particularly experienced servicemen, treated the whole idea of ghosts as a joke, not to be taken seriously, until they found themselves facing an apparition.

Around the same period as John Wears met the 'Orderly Officer', two such servicemen were on guard duty out on the airfield itself.

They were required to check on the mortuary, a duty that, because of its morbid associations, was generally completed as quickly as possible. On that particular night they also had to check on a plane standing near the now demolished control tower, which was situated opposite the mortuary.

The pair were bored and, with nothing much happening, they took it in turns to disappear to a quiet corner for a smoke break.

In the early hours of the morning, the solitary guard left on patrol near the mortuary was shocked when its doors suddenly burst open, not least of all because he had only just checked and found them to be locked.

A figure, with a deathly pale face, dressed in full flying kit, emerged through the open doors and walked towards the terrified guard. The guard was so shocked that he dropped his rifle and, just as he bent down to retrieve it, the figure vanished. There was then a loud bang as the doors of the mortuary clanged shut, followed only by a deathly stillness.

When his colleague returned from his break the still shaken guard made no mention of the incident, although he did wonder to himself whether he had been the subject of a particularly tasteless practical joke.

It was only years later, when discussing RAF Montrose with another former RAF man who had served there, that he learned that the mortuary building had previously been used as a dispersal hut and it had been from there that the Flight Lieutenant had walked out to make his final, fatal flight.

One of the Few

At least one ghost with a Montrose connection actually appeared several hundred miles away in Harrogate.

Noel 'Broody' Benson was one of the pilots of 603 squadron which was stationed at RAF Montrose during the early summer of 1940. During that time, German reconnaissance planes and bombers flew missions over the north-east of Scotland and the pilots of 603 squadron were sent to intercept them in what has been called the Battle of Scotland.

Benson was born in North Yorkshire in 1918. His love of flying was due to his father who had apparently organised a flying trip for the family from Montrose to York. The flight itself was, apparently, somewhat uncomfortable due to air turbulence and, although his mother and sister were not particularly impressed by the experience, Noel and his brother Brian both enjoyed themselves thoroughly and Noel in particular was smitten by the idea of flying as a career.

In April 1938, he enrolled at RAF Cranwell as a flight cadet and after his passing out parade he spent some time at Croydon before being posted to Montrose.

On 22nd July 1940 he was the pilot of one of three Spitfires who encountered and were responsible for shooting down a Dornier Do 17P 75 miles east of Aberdeen.

A month later, 603 Squadron were sent south to Hornchurch in the south-east of England where the Battle of Britain was at its height.

At 18.36 on 28th August 1940 eleven Spitfires took off from Hornchurch for the last patrol of the day. Just over an hour and a half later, ten Spitfires returned. The missing plane was Benson's who was initially reported missing.

Benson's Spitfire had been attacked by Messerschmitt 109s and crashed in flames near the hamlet of Leigh Green.

In July, his aircraft had been damaged over the North Sea but on that occasion he had been able to fly his stricken aircraft back to Montrose. Unfortunately, luck was not with him this time.

Even in death however the young pilot had done his duty, struggling to ensure his burning plane missed the small clump of houses below him.

Obviously, his family were devastated but his sister Margaret later told of a strange experience which had given some comfort to herself and her mother.

The two women had been walking down a street in Harrogate when they saw three RAF airmen on the pavement across the road from them.

Although neither mentioned it to the other, each woman, and remember we are talking about close relatives here, had the unshakeable belief that the middle man of the group was Noel!

Through Youthful Eyes

A number of strange happenings at the former RAF Montrose have been reported by children and young people. Often these seem to take place on evenings when there is a light covering of mist over the airfield.

The former airfield, with its open space and old air raid shelters and buildings, many now sadly gone, has always provided an attractive play area for children.

One particular evening two children were playing there. They noticed a figure some way away but they carried on with their games, taking no real notice of it.

As they played they became aware that the figure was coming in their direction but that was not what unnerved them however.

Other than the old concrete perimeter track, the surface of the airfield is now generally rough, covered with tufts of grass which make the surface uneven and difficult to walk steadily on, yet the figure was having no difficulty in moving, being described by the children as 'gliding towards them', as if on rails.

Unsurprisingly, the children did not linger.

Another such incident involved two older children. They too saw a figure coming towards them through the mist.

Being older, they were perhaps more sure of themselves and they made no attempt to leave.

It was only when the figure got close enough for them to see that it had no features, only a blank space where its face should have been, did they take to their heels and run.

Some people appear to have an ability to see things that other do not. Another odd happening involved four young women who were in a car being driven through the area between the old WWII hangar and the area now occupied by the vehicle testing station.

Three of the occupants suddenly became hysterical, claiming that they could see some sort of apparition, while the fourth young woman saw nothing unusual and could not understand why her friends were so upset.

A local woman was in the habit of walking her Alsatian dog on the airfield in the early morning.

One particular day, the dog was exercising as usual when suddenly it stopped some way away and looked back towards her with its hackles raised.

Just then, the woman heard a voice saying, "I'm here".

The woman looked around but could see no one. Initially, she thought it was someone hiding in the whin bushes playing a practical joke on her.

She heard the words "I'm here" again, loudly this time, as if the speaker was standing beside her.

If there had been someone hiding nearby she was convinced that she would have been aware of them as she would have heard the bushes moving.

As she hurried away she heard the voice again, still repeating its strange message.

Technical Fault – Ghostly Solution?

During the winter of 1940/41, a detachment from 111 Squadron was based at RAF Montrose. Among the ground crew stationed there was LAC 'Crash' Symonds and this is his ghost story.

One afternoon during the spring of 1941, a Hurricane from B Flight landed and taxied towards the dispersal point but, for some unknown reason, the engine suddenly cut out without warning.

Now the only way to move a Hurricane was by hand but this one was some distance out and the surface was fairly rough. Montrose had only three grass runways covered in wire, so the decision was taken to take a trolley accumulator starter out to the plane and restart the engine.

As Symonds and the rest of his ground crew made their way to the stricken aircraft they met the pilot who told them he would come back to taxi the aircraft back to the dispersal point after he had reported to the Flight Commander.

Once the ground crew reached the stranded Hurricane they plugged the starter trolley in and started to carry out the procedures required to restart the engine. Corporal Radcliffe climbed into the cockpit and Symonds took responsibility for the starter trolley button.

On the given signal, both Radcliffe and Symonds pressed their respective buttons and the propeller started to turn but the engine steadfastly refused to start.

The procedure was repeated several times without success until the battery on the starter trolley was absolutely flat.

Nothing more could be done and the group started to trudge back towards the dispersal point discussing possible causes of the failure of the engine to catch.

They had only gone about 20 yards when they suddenly heard the engine burst into life. But even as they turned and ran towards the Hurricane the engine stopped again.

Sergeant Trotter was the first to reach the aircraft and he climbed onto the plane only to report that there was no one in the cockpit.

Trotter carried out a full check of the cockpit but all was as it should have been in that all the switches were off, the fuel switch was off and the throttle closed.

Totally surprised by this turn of events the airmen had a quick discussion before deciding to try to start the engine again. The starter trolley was plugged in again, the necessary cockpit routine repeated and this time, much to everyone's surprise, the engine roared into life.

The pilot, having completed his debriefing returned to his aircraft and taxied back to the dispersal point and all seemed to return to normal.

But for LAC Symonds many questions were never answered. He couldn't understand why the engine wouldn't start initially and how it came to start on its own with a starter trolley powered by an apparently flat battery.

Various theories have been put forward but 'Crash' wasn't convinced by any of them. Perhaps, he always felt, only the ghost pilot of Montrose really knew the answer.

Members' Experiences

All that remains today of RFC/RAF Montrose buildings is the former headquarters, now occupied by the Montrose Air Station Heritage Centre which commemorates the history of Britain's first operational airfield, and a number of First and Second War hangars.

Many of the members have had personal experiences of strange occurrences and David Butler tells two similar tales.

Not long after the present Centre building had been purchased, David was working there along with his son Neil, another member. The building was in a poor state of repair and a considerable amount of work was required to bring it up to standard so that the public could be admitted.

David was working in the old Commanding Officer's office while Neil was busy further through the building. At one point, David was suddenly aware of a shadow passing by one of the windows. He told me that it was a fine sunny day and there was no likely explanation or cause of the shadow.

On another occasion, another member, Ian Robb, was working in the Centre. By that time, the former CO's office had been fitted out much as it would have been during WWII.

David had procured a telephone from the War period and it had been set up in the office, although it was not connected up in any way.

Ian Robb heard the phone ring and when he picked it he could hear a voice "Asking for help".

Strangely enough, when David investigated the source of the telephone he found that it had come from Stracathro Hospital, near Brechin, where it had been used in a ward that had treated injured airmen.

Another member, John Melville, was approached by a middle aged couple one day who said they were looking for information on their son's period of service at RAF Montrose.

Without giving the matter much thought he pointed out a relevant group photograph and left to do something else. When he went back to look for them the couple had disappeared. It was only when he remarked to someone else on the fact that the parents had vanished so quickly, and it was pointed out that the airman would then have been in his eighties so his parents would presumably have had to be centenarians, that he realised that his visitors were perhaps not what they seemed.

I spent a number of summers working as a Development Officer at the Centre. It was common to hear what sounded like footsteps echoing through the wooden building but, invariably, further investigation revealed that there was no one there.

On one occasion however, I did have an experience that I could not explain. I was showing the Stirnimann family from Switzerland around the Centre. The talk came round to the number of ghosts and we chatted about the various stories.

When they decided to leave I found that the bolt on the outside of the door had engaged.

We were able to leave by one of the other doors and I discovered that the bolt had moved just enough to lock us in.

There were other people in the building but none of them had been outside. Certainly, there was a wind that day but while I would imagine the wind might move the door and make the bolt loosen I find it hard to believe that it made the bolt engage.

Perhaps it was one of the many RAF Montrose ghosts reminding me that their memory should be treated with respect!

Recent Sightings

During the time I have been researching this book there have been further ghost experiences at RAF Montrose.

The Centre regularly hosts military vehicle weekends when owners of military vehicles come together with other enthusiasts.

Often, the participants enter into the spirit of the weekend by dressing in an appropriate uniform to go with their particular vehicle.

At a recent re-enactment event, one of the ladies who had attended along with her husband needed to use the toilet during the night.

When such events are on, the participants are generally allowed to use the toilet facilities at the north end of the Heritage Centre building during the night. On this occasion, the lady decided to use the toilet through the main building at the other end of the Centre.

To get there, she had to pass through the main exhibition room where, in the semi darkness, she noticed two men in RAF uniform standing chatting in a corner. Perhaps spurred on by the urgency of her own 'mission', she paid little attention to them and continued to the toilet area. When she returned the figures had disappeared.

At first she thought they were two of the enthusiasts, perhaps playing a trick on her.

It was only when she realised that all the men were accounted for outside that it dawned on her that she had seen two of the station's ghosts.

The other incident is even more bizarre. A mother and son visiting the Centre went to see the introductory video which gives visitors some of the background to the history of the air base at Montrose.

The lady, who seemed to have considerable clairvoyant powers from some of the things she was able to tell one of the members on duty, mentioned how all the seats in the room had been taken but one of the airmen had kindly risen up and given her his.

Of course, there are no airmen based at RAF Montrose these days, so the gentleman, polite though he may have been, was certainly not what he seemed!

> The Montrose Air Station Heritage Centre, which is situated at the north end of the town, is open most days during the summer, Sundays throughout the year and at other times by arrangement. Confirmation of opening times can be obtained from the website <www.rafmontrose.org.uk> or by telephoning 01674 678222.

The House of Dun   OS map, sheet 54: NO 670599

In common with so many of the big houses or castles in the area, the House of Dun, home to the Erskine family, later the Kennedy-Erskines, for almost six hundred years, has its share of ghost stories.

Today, the House of Dun, which is situated to the north of the A935 midway between Brechin and Montrose, belongs to the National Trust for Scotland. William Adam built the current house for David Erskine, Lord Dun, in the year 1730.

Before that, the Erskine family lived in Dun Castle which is believed to have occupied a site close to the present building.

Probably the best known of the Erskine family was the fifth Laird of Dun, John Erskine, 1509–1589. The fifth Laird was one of the most important participants in the Scottish Reformation, making a contribution rivalled only by John Knox himself.

But even the saintly fifth Laird had his moments of notoriety. In his youth he had murdered a catholic priest in the bell tower of the Church in Montrose and for that crime he had to pay compensation to the dead man's family.

If the fifth Laird is the most famous member of the family then Robert Erskine is undoubtedly the most infamous.

During the early part of the seventeenth century, Robert Erskine and his three sisters, Annas, Isobel and Helen, attempted to murder their nephew John Erskine, the tenth Laird, and his brother, Alexander, in an attempt to allow Robert to inherit the estate.

To achieve their foul objective they gave the two boys ale laced with poisonous herbs which made both boys seriously ill and eventually, after several months, John died.

Alexander, however, survived to become the eleventh laird and for their wicked crime, Robert, Isobel and Annas were executed and Helen was banished from the kingdom.

In fact, it is just possible that the boys' illnesses were brought about by naturally occurring mould found on grain but there is no real evidence to support that theory.

Anyway, given the colourful history of the family it is not at all surprising that the House itself appears to have its share of ghosts, although, strangely enough, none appear to relate to the earlier history of the family.

Mary Brownlow, who was the House Manager for a spell in the early noughties, has some interesting stories to tell.

One night, Mary's husband Ian was awakened by the sound of voices which was surprising to say the least as there was no one else in the House except himself and Mary.

On another occasion, again when there was no else there, Mary heard a baby crying. The sound went on for at least three-quarters of an hour and, although Mary searched for the origins of the noise and investigated other possible causes, she could find no plausible explanation.

At one point, Mary was talking to someone on the telephone when she heard another phone ringing. When she finished her call she went to check out the mystery telephone. As she went upstairs she could hear the phone still ringing – only there is no telephone in that part of the House.

Mary had wondered if perhaps there was another telephone, long since lost in a cupboard perhaps, but still connected, or some other logical explanation. There was none.

A BT engineer was called to investigate and he checked the system but he could find no trace of a hidden instrument.

Previous House Managers, upstairs in their private accommodation, have heard music from the salon and this has been confirmed by other members of staff.

On the Dun estate there are flats which are let out to visitors (**7**). One family described in the visitors' book how their two little girls had seen a dress, without any head or feet, float through their room, while visitors to the House itself have reported seeing a white figure with a bonnet on the top landing.

7 *The Ghost Club investigation at House of Dun.*

Karen Ritchie experienced many visions as a child and thought it was perfectly normal when she regularly saw a lady at the foot of her bed. It was only when she was living in Germany that she realised she had a special gift which encouraged her to join a spiritualist circle where she was able to develop her skills.

In 2005, Karen visited the House of Dun with her friend Pauline, another medium, to make arrangements for her wedding.

Mary Brownlow was standing with the two women in Mr Kennedy's parlour when Karen became aware of the presence of a little girl, dressed in dark clothes and long black hair that hung in ringlets down to the middle of her back, happily skipping around the group.

She then stood close to the three women for a spell before finally skipping away.

Initially, Karen was concerned about mentioning her sighting but when she described her vision to Mary she did not dismiss her claims.

Upstairs, in the green parlour, Pauline felt uncomfortable and had to leave but Karen felt perfectly at ease and said she could hear women's voices speaking French

In another of the public rooms, Karen could hear incessant chatter, similar, she told me, to being in a busy pub. There was no music, just the sound of men's voices although she was unable to make out any individual words. She also experienced an overpowering smell, like a mixture of pipe and cigar smoke. It was certainly not the smell of cigarettes.

In one of the bedrooms Karen became aware of a lady's presence, a lady of quality with very erect posture, she felt.

Karen believed that this woman resented the visitors' presence as she felt they had no right to be there in her personal space.

Upstairs, Karen 'met' an austere looking gentleman in very dark clothing. He looked particularly stern and she felt he was obviously used to giving orders and criticising.

Most activity however, was centred on the basement. There, for example, Karen experienced dogs scratching at the doors and running around their feet. She described them as friendly, happy dogs with no intention of hurting anyone.

When they moved towards the kitchen Mary opened the door and stood back to allow Karen and Pauline go in first. Karen said she had difficulty when she tried to enter the room, almost as if some strong force was preventing her from doing so.

As well as having to force her way in, Karen described the room as being cold and unwelcoming, despite the fact that the temperature in the House is strictly regulated.

Just as she reached the bottom of the steps she became aware of the cook standing in the far corner of the room. At one point, the cook clapped her hands and Karen could see the cloud of flour that resulted. Karen felt that this woman was a frightening presence who did not take kindly to 'intruders' in her space. Subsequent research by Mary found that a Miss Peddie, a lady who had a reputation for being bossy and stern, had worked in the kitchen in the early part of last century. The cook was not the only presence in the basement who made the visitors unwelcome as the ladies later 'met' a manservant, whom they thought was possibly called Albert, who told them in no uncertain terms to get out.

In the little theatre, Karen was aware of a couthy, easy going old gentleman leaning on the fireplace smoking his pipe while, in another room, she experienced a dark haired man in a suit. She formed the impression that his name was David, as distinct from Dave or Davie.

As the two women were leaving the House, Karen looked out through the glass doors where she could see a black carriage drawn by two beautifully groomed black horses. Instinctively, Karen knew that it was going to Montrose but she was surprised to see it head north, away from the House, rather than travelling around the property and up the drive to the main road.

With some hesitation she told Mary of this particular vision and was surprised to be told that originally the main road had been on that side of the House so that it would have been normal at one time for travellers to leave in the direction she had described.

Karen sensed two further things. Firstly, she believed that at some point the stables had caught fire, as she was aware of frightened horses and a time of panic.

Secondly, she felt the presence of a woman who had grieved all her life over the death of her first born child. Whether the baby was stillborn or whether it died in infancy Karen couldn't tell but she believed it was a boy. The lady later had two girls but Karen felt she never recovered from the loss of that first child.

A Ghost Tour

Mary had organised a ghost evening as a means of boosting visitor numbers and she was so impressed by Karen and Pauline's abilities that she invited them to take part.

The two ladies agreed but, before the tour started, Mary began to have second thoughts about having mediums present and she asked them to stay in Mr Kennedy's parlour while she asked the members of the tour party if they were agreeable to having them there. The visitors were happy to have the two ladies on the tour so Karen and Pauline joined the main party.

In the meantime however, Mary's husband had heard voices coming from the parlour. He was surprised to hear a conversation taking place between Karen and Pauline and the Lady of the House who was less than pleased about all the visitors who had invaded her property. Mary stressed to me later that Karen and Pauline were not aware that anyone was listening to them

Towards the end of the tour, as the party had gathered in the kitchen, Karen and Pauline had stayed close to the door since the presence there, perhaps Miss Peddie, had made it clear they were not welcome. A member of the group, who was standing beside a chair, exactly at the spot where the two mediums had first become aware of the presence in the kitchen, suddenly burst into tears for no apparent reason.

Another member had become separated from the tour party. Mary went to look for her and the two almost bumped into each other as the lady ran out of the theatre. Like Karen and her friend earlier, she had encountered Albert who had told her to get out!

Mary did consider whether it was all a set-up but her investigations revealed that the lady involved had only just arrived in this country and had no knowledge of either the two women or the history of the House.

Sometime later I was present with the members of the Ghost Club (8) when they carried out an investigation at Dun which produced some interesting results which appeared to confirm similar paranormal activity, although apart from coordinator Derek Green, the members present that evening had no knowledge of Karen's findings.

At one point my own group had formed a circle and, at different points, each one of us was pulled towards the east, as if someone or something was tugging us in that direction.

The House of Dun is open during the tourist season although the gardens and estate are open all year round. Further details can be obtained from the website <www.nts.org.uk> or by telephoning 0844 493 2144.

8 *The Ghost Club seeking evidence of the paranormal at Dun.*

Meddling With the Unknown

The Dun estate itself has been the scene of a number of strange happenings.

A report in the *Montrose Review* of 4th January 1850 tells of the 'Haunted House of Dun'.

Often I listened to the old people relating how the district swains and timorous maidens would "ha'e gane a mile about an mair" before they would have transversed the gloomy bypaths and haunted hedgerows of Dun after nightfall, lest they should chance to meet with the aerial rider, commonly called the "headless huntsman" who was said to gallop nightly in that locality.

Another folk tale tells of two employees who lived in the West Lodges and how they fell foul of supernatural forces.

They were working on what is left of the old Kirk of Dun, now a mausoleum, when they found two gold coloured candlesticks and decided to keep one each.

When one employee got home his wife refused to allow him to keep the candlestick in the house, demanding that he bury it outside and then return it to its rightful place the following day.

The other worker kept his candlestick in the house and his family was kept awake all night by howling sounds and banging noises. He too, returned the candlestick the next morning.

Another spirit that reputedly haunts the Dun estate is that of a woman, riding, facing backwards, on a horse.

According to legend she had been unfaithful to her husband while he was away fighting. Her punishment was to be hanged and she was taken to her execution on a horse in the manner described, which was supposed to be a sign of disgrace.

Somewhere on the Dun estate, there is believed to be a carving that depicts the scene.

Another Montrose Ghost

Almost forty years after announcing the legend of the headless horseman the Review carried another ghost story. The issue dated 23th September 1887 advised:

> A rumour got abroad in the beginning of the week that someone had seen what he or she supposed to be a ghost in the neighbourhood of St Peter's Chapel. As a result a crowd of several young people assembled in the neighbourhood on Thursday night and hung about for a considerable time, but had to disperse without seeing anything of the ghostly visitor. On Wednesday night a similar crowd assembled at the same place, but they were also disappointed. So far as could be ascertained nothing has been seen to give rise to the foolish rumour.

Strangely enough, I came across the following piece in *A Gable Ender's Gossip* by Bob Mackie, written in 1951, which I suspect actually describes the same incident.

> An old lady told how in her teens a ghost appeared in Chapel Lane (Place) for two nights.
> The lane was so crowded that the police had to clear the way and a few of the tenants in it became, by the alarm, quite demented. The ghost was

said to be clothed in white, made no noise, moved with an amazing swiftness, and sprang up nearby trees where, among the leaves, it made queer and frightening sounds. The police declared that they did not see anything resembling a ghost and the old lady said that she saw nothing but there were some who persisted long in believing that there was absolute truth in the story.

Lauriston Castle

OS map, sheet 45: NO 761666

Lauriston Castle is actually near St Cyrus in Kincardineshire but the following tale is an intriguing one which may be part of the RAF Montrose story.

The first record of a castle on this site was in 1243 and since then it has gone through several incarnations and been in the ownership of several families.

It was while it belonged to the Straton family that one of the most bizarre incidents in Scottish history occurred.

Some of the local barons in the Mearns (the area of an old Pictish kingdom which is now the county of Kincardineshire), were unhappy with the behaviour of Sheriff Melville who was the King's representative in the area. They complained to the King about his arrogant actions and, in response, the King casually replied that he didn't care if they "biled the loon and suppit the bree" (boiled him and drank the juice).

Taking the King at his word the barons invited Melville to a hunting party near Lauriston where they tipped him into a cauldron of boiling water before drinking the resultant soup.

The King was not pleased as he hadn't intended his words to be taken literally so the conspirators were forced to flee for a time, although they managed to avoid real punishment and the Straton family remained in control of Lauriston.

During the first half of the 16th century, another member of the family found himself in trouble although this time he was unable to avoid the consequences.

David Stratoun, the spelling had changed over time, was fishing for salmon near St Cyrus when he was asked by the local priest, the Vicar of Ecclesgreig, to hand over every tenth fish he caught to the Church in payment of the teinds, a tax of one tenth of income, similar to tithes.

Stratoun was a particularly headstrong young man and he promptly ordered that every tenth of the fish caught be thrown back into the sea, saying that if the Church wanted them they could get them in the same way that he did.

As a result of his actions he had to appear before the Church authorities but he was unwilling to recant, his argument being about the Church's grasping ways rather than any heretical thought. He was burnt at the stake for his stubbornness.

A few years ago, a ghost incident occurred when a party of school-children were visiting the Castle. They had been shown the tower and the rest of the building including the courtyard which is surrounded by a very high wall.

Before long, it was time to return to school but, when the teacher called them together to make sure that they were all accounted for, she discovered that one young girl was missing.

When the girl was eventually found she explained that she had been in the courtyard talking to a man who had been sitting on the high stone wall, although no one else had seen the figure.

When asked to describe the man she said he was wearing a funny leather helmet with flaps down over the ears. As she continued her story, it became apparent to the listeners that she appeared to be describing someone wearing early flying gear.

Although the little girl had never heard of Desmond Arthur many of the people present were convinced that he was the figure she had seen.

No record exists of any connection with the old Montrose air station, although it was not unusual for the early flyers to land, or be forced to land, on any stretch of grass they could find, so they often appeared in the unlikeliest of places and, of course, crashes, often fatal, were commonplace.

Certainly, the Castle was requisitioned by the RAF in 1940 for use as a barracks for RAF Montrose and its satellite airfields so it may be that the person the little girl was speaking to came from a later period than anyone thought.

There could however be another explanation as another pilot had connections with the area.

Shelia Watson was a quiet young woman from Stonehaven who had been brought up in a very strict working class family. Her life changed however when she met a dashing young farmer from the Mearns called Max Garvie at a dance in Stonehaven Town Hall in January 1953.

Within 18 months they were married and Sheila went to live at the Garvie farm at West Cairnbeg near Laurencekirk.

She found the change in her life difficult to deal with, not least because of the actions of the free spending, hard drinking young farmer.

Garvie was a man who appeared to have everything; money, an attractive wife and his own private plane all contributed to a lifestyle that other people envied.

The reality however was very different and behind the glamour there were serious tensions between Garvie and his wife Sheila.

In May 1968, Garvie, who, after developing his interest in flying, was sometimes referred to as 'the flying farmer', was reported missing.

Some months later, in mid August, the body of Max Garvie was found in one of the underground tunnels close to Laurieston Castle and Sheila Garvie and the man who had become her lover, Brain Tevendale, were immediately arrested.

Joining the lovers in the dock was Alan Peters, a friend of Tevendale's. At the pleading diet, Sheila Garvie's agent lodged a motion that the defence would attack her husband's character 'in respect of his unnatural and perverted sexual practices'.

Mrs Garvie and Peters also lodged notices of special defences, with Mrs Garvie effectively claiming that the murder had been carried out by her two co-accused, while Peters, who denied murdering Garvie, claimed that he had been coerced into taking part by Tevendale.

Otherwise, the three accused all entered pleas of Not Guilty.

The Trial

The trial, which started on Tuesday 19th November, was held in the High Court in Aberdeen.

A mixture of salacious rumour and Mrs Garvie's motion meant that there was huge interest in the trial and each day, members of the public queued outside the Court from early morning hoping to get a seat in the public gallery.

What followed was one of the most talked about cases in Scottish legal history, with spectacular revelations appearing in the press reports most mornings.

The trial largely lived up to the tabloid press's expectations, with tales of a nudist colony in Aberdeenshire at a house which the locals had quickly dubbed 'kinky cottage'. There were allegations too of abnormal sexual demands by Max Garvie on his wife, of her being forced into a relationship with Brian Tevendale by her husband who, it was also suggested, was bi-sexual.

But, despite the allegation that their relationship had initially been to satisfy one of Garvie's fantasies, Sheila and Brian Tevendale had fallen in love and the result was tragic.

Whether Max Garvie was guilty of the 'offences' he was being accused of is impossible to say. He was not on trial and consequently, as has been pointed out by several observers, had no defence team to argue for his reputation.

The fact of the matter however was that he had been murdered and the jury had to decide whether all or any of the accused had carried out the dark deed.

The Crown case was that on the night of 14/15th May, Tevendale and Peters had arrived at West Cairnbeg and Garvie was shot at close range as he slept. The pair then dragged the body downstairs to Peters' car which was used to move the body to Lauriston.

Guilty!

After ten days of evidence the jury were unanimous in finding Tevendale Guilty while Sheila Garvie was found Guilty on a majority verdict and the case against Peters Not Proven.

Tevendale and Sheila Garvie were both sentenced to life imprisonment. Some locals believe that the figure in flying gear sometimes seen at Lauriston Castle is not a pilot from the airfield at Montrose but Max Garvie looking to salvage his lost reputation.

There is another strange episode relating to the tragedy. From the outset, Sheila Garvie consistently argued that she played no part in the murder of her husband and that she had no prior knowledge of Tevendale's intentions that night.

On her release from prison she wrote a book giving her side of the story. In it she tells of how her mother, a spiritualist, had cried at her wedding and gone a deathly shade of white. They were not, she realised even then, tears of joy. In fact she suspects her mother may have had a premonition.

Did Mrs Watson have at least an inkling of the tragic event that would end in her son-in-law's death and her daughter's imprisonment? It is an intriguing thought.

But there is more to Lauriston castle than the ghost of an airman. A resident, sleeping in one of the front rooms was awakened by someone putting a hand over their mouth. There was no one else in the room.

There have been sightings too of figures from earlier history. An apprentice plumber working on the refurbishment of the property of the Castle saw a figure with a white beard, dressed in white, standing beside the hedge. It then disappeared.

Spirits Keeping In Touch

Often the image people have of ghosts is of spirits dragging chains or of one of Henry VIII's wives with her head tucked underneath her arm but ghosts have moved into the 21st century and so have those looking for proof of their existence.

One very modern investigator is Montrose woman Cat Perks who investigates what is known as white or pink noise.

Cat uses voice recorders and video cameras to capture messages from the afterlife, although any electronic medium, such as computers, telephones, mobiles, radios or digital voice recorders, can be used.

It was in the spring of 2006 that Cat first became aware that her late mother had been contacting her through home videos and had also made contact by mobile phone.

The first occasion, when her mother asked, "Are you OK?", was, Cat says, hair raising to say the least.

Two days later, she contacted Cat on her mobile and said ,"Listen". The call lasted some six and a half minutes, although Cat admits she couldn't always catch what was being said.

Later, her mother sent her a voicemail message.

Cat has recordings of her mother saying, "Catherine waiting at hospital. Was seeing grand-dad."

Eventually, Cat discovered that if she asked questions she would get answers. Asked about grand-dad the voice said, "Yes, he crossed over". On another occasion, someone spoke on behalf of her grand-dad, "Must leave this earth. Laugh Cathy." (Cat was called Cathy by the family.)

Cat had been estranged from her family for a number of years and the last time she spoke to her grand-dad, he was in his early nineties, and didn't know her.

The recordings include other massages such as, "Dinnae mean this – Go back will you". (Although that was not delivered by her grand-dad, Cat assumes it was a request from him to remember happy times.)

Wanting to know about her grandfather, Cat telephoned a cousin whom she had last spoken to in 2002, to ask about him.

She was told that he had passed away down in England. He had been cremated and the ashes were to be scattered in Scotland, although her cousin didn't know if that had been done.

Cat says she was angry to hear of her grandfather's death from the spirit world.

Just a few days later Cat recorded her grand-dad whistling and saying, "I'm in another world". She has since had lots of recordings and believes her grand-dad is keeping an eye on family members.

Cat's mother seems to use Cat's mobile to get in contact and Cat has also had a male American voice announcing, "Warm-hearted greetings – nice to meet you Cat."

Other people also seem to contact Cat using this medium, including the voice of a friend saying, "I'm always here".

In August 2008 Cat visited the former headquarters building at RAF Montrose for an investigation conducted using her instruments and her own perceptive senses.

Her research produced a number of interesting results with Cat experiencing the sound of footsteps, like men in heavy boots marching, in the hallway.

In other areas, such as the former Commanding Officer's room, she experienced unusually cold spots, while in the most northerly room she found herself choking to the point where she was almost rendered unconscious, which led her to believe she had encountered the spirit of an airman who had died in a crash.

Her recordings also produced snatches of conversation and she believes she also made contact with an airman called Arthur, although she doesn't believe that he was Desmond Arthur.

Another encounter was with an airman whom she was able to describe in some detail; square type face, dark hair, tall medium build, possibly called Jackson.

Possibly the most important conclusion Cat came to however was the fact that there are certainly spirits present at the former airfield.

Sea Monsters

Over the centuries, sea faring communities have been obsessed with the idea of sea monsters, those fearsome creatures of the deep that they believed were responsible for sinking ships and consuming unwary sailors.

At the beginning of the 20th century, the Angus coast near Montrose was apparently something of a hot spot for sea serpents or monsters.

Early on the morning of Friday 4th September 1903, George Johnston, first engineer, David Nicol, first fisherman and David Wilson, another hand, all crew members on the Montrose fishing boat *Rosa*, saw a large shape above the water about a mile away.

The creature was in sight for approximately 15 minutes so they had no doubt about what they had seen and were able to watch in fascination, as the monster, which they described as being of 'distinctly snakey appearance', continued swimming in a northerly direction.

Its head rose out of the water for some five or six feet and then, about a boat-length behind, 'a larger and curved-like portion' could be seen above the water and behind that, a further smaller portion of the creature.

The animal would dive for a short period before re-appearing again – 'in the same form' as before. 'The uncanny-looking animal made no noise, and apparently swam at great speed.'

The incident was reported in the *Montrose Review* but the other local newspaper, the *Montrose Standard*, poured scorn on the tale, suggesting that such stories were part of the 'silly season' and in keeping with 'big gooseberries and other oddities'.

The writer suggested, a bit like sceptics on the subjects of big cats or UFOs today, that crews should have a camera ready so that they could produce real evidence.

A Monstrous Sight

Strangely enough, the next description of a sea monster appeared in the correspondence column of the *Standard* in August of the following year when a letter writer, styling himself 'Seaman', wrote an account of his terrifying encounter with a huge monster while crossing the old suspension bridge over the River South Esk (**9**).

9 *The old Suspension Bridge at Montrose was said to be the scene of an attack by a sea monster.*

Seaman described himself as an old sailor who had weathered many latitudes 'but never saw a specimen of the great sea serpent until last Sunday evening about a quarter to twelve'.

As the Seaman, accompanied by his eldest son and a nephew, reached the middle of the bridge there was

> a terrific concussion. There was a loud yet muffled bump, as if something of a fleshy nature had struck the bridge from below. There was an ear-splitting yell, like the sound of a herd of angry swine, and then there was a very heavy splash. The bridge was quivering all over, and we were trembling in unison, when a huge shadow rose up on the east of the structure. We soon saw that it was the head of a gigantic monster, serpent-like in shape and with that deadly malignity of expression that belongs to the snake tribe.

Seaman continued that the trio were rooted to the spot as the head of the brute, 'as large as an ordinary cab', tried in vain to reach them. He believed that the serpent blamed his group for the pain caused to it by its accidental collision with the bridge.

As far as he could tell, the beast stretched back down the river for some three or four hundred yards and 'rose and fell in a number of horrible undulations'.

The terrified trio crouched in a corner as the giant head, 'its huge eyes glaring with wrath', continued its attempts to attack them. As it did so, they could hear the click of his massive tusks, and feel 'the mephitic odour of his breath'.

According to the Seaman's account, only the monster's dimensions prevented it venting its wrath on the cowering figures as the beast tried to get at them, the chains and railings of the bridge baulking its efforts.

> At last, with a valedictory howl of blood-curdling fury, he turned tail and dashed out to sea at a high speed.

Unsurprisingly, the three took to their heels and ran off, the Seaman forgetting his age and rheumatism as he and his companions sought safety on the shore.

A Great Debate

The Seaman's point was that the residents of the town should be protected from such monsters. He reminded readers that just a few years before another such specimen had appeared off the nearby fishing village of Ferryden, much to the consternation of the local population.

Small firearms he reckoned would be no use against such a beast but 'a heavy shell from one of the heavy guns now used by our Militia and Volunteer Artillery might do execution'.

He felt that people were too keen to mock such happenings, treating even well documented sightings as if they were a myth when in fact incidents such as he described were no laughing matter.

The main result of the story was a flurry of correspondence, which ranged in tone from the supportive to the critical and mocking, to the letters' pages of the local press.

One writer, calling himself 'Fisherman', queried the description and pointed out that it lacked accuracy. He even took the unfortunate Seaman to task over the monster's intentions. Fisherman claimed to have also had a brief encounter with such a beast and his experience led him to believe that, in all probability, it had been rubbing itself against the bridge to remove parasites.

On a more positive note he saw the monster as a possible tourist attraction writing; 'the existence of such a creature in our neighbourhood or even the chance of an occasional visit from it, would add to the attractiveness of our town'.

Another letter writer, a mother visiting the town, took a rather different view. She had come to the Burgh with her husband and children for a month's rest and found all the talk of the monster upsetting for her young family.

This time it was the turn of the *Montrose Review* to doubt the sea monster story. It published a letter from D U Twig of Usan which explained that the London papers had taken different views on the subject. The *Daily Mail* had reproduced the tale 'in all seriousness', while the *Daily News* had 'made game of the "Sea Serpent" at Montrose hoax'.

Twig reckoned he could explain the genesis of the "Sea Serpent" which, he wrote, 'is one of a species not unknown in Montrose, and is said to hail from the neighbourhood of the Auld Kirk of Logie-Pert', a nearby hamlet.

Logie-Pert was blessed with an Auld Kirk but it is more likely that Twig was using the old Scot's euphemism for whisky. He continued in this vein by suggesting, after a number of Biblical references, that 'seeing "serpents" is generally the sequel to spirituous experiences'.

His letter ended:

> Some who are not Biblical authorities think that the gentleman who signs himself "seaman" might have been better occupied had he been conducting family worship, instead of trying to "fleg" [frighten] canny Montrosians with a fairy tale.

If Twig found the whole episode humorous then others were still impressed by the Seaman's story. J Douglas Straight of Musselburgh wrote that initially he had thought Seaman was 'half seas over, and out of his latitude'.

On reflection however he had decided that as Seaman had his two witnesses there could be no doubt about the truth of his story. He also pointed out that around two years before there had been a similar tale printed in the columns of the *Standard*.

That sighting had led him to hope that some scientific research might result but none had been forthcoming.

Writing from the safety of his own home he queried the Seaman's inability to fully describe the monster's appearance by detailing such things as, scales, colour, build etc. before conceding:

> One must suppose that the fearful agony experienced by the writer kept him from seeing what a naturalist would readily have observed. It must be satisfactory, however, to the authorities concerned that the Suspension Bridge has railings and chains so powerful as to defy all the efforts of a sea serpent, even though its head be as big as a cab and its length three hundred feet.

Comforting as that thought might have been for the authorities it would have been of little comfort to the unfortunate Seaman, provided of course, that his letter was not simply a gigantic hoax.

On the other hand, given the time of his sighting, perhaps he had indeed had a 'spirituous' experience.

A Spirited Landlady

The Ferryden Hotel, later known as the Esk Hotel, has been a watering hole for villagers and tourists over many years. Its most famous landlady was Mrs Lily Winchester and the pub itself was known to everyone in the area as Diamond Lil's.

Lil had been serving drinks at the Esk since she and her husband took over the hotel in the early 1950s. She was something of a character and, while she was a great Royalist and defender of women's rights, she was not above cocking a snoot at the authorities when the mood took her.

The introduction of decimal money in the UK was something that Lil strongly disapproved of and she waged her own, one-woman, campaign against the 'new-fangled' coinage.

She claimed she didn't understand decimal currency but actually understood it, or at least the conversion of old to new money, better than most. Her response was quite simple, she ignored it.

Buy a round of drinks in Lil's and she would inform you that it came to say £2 3s.4d. Now within a short time of decimalisation being introduced, no one, apart from Lil that is, ever thought of money in those terms.

So, customers handed over a larger amount and waited for change. If someone had passed Lil £5 for that round she would have handed back their change, in decimal coinage, counting out a mixture of new coinage to make up, by her reckoning, the £2 16s.8d. required as change.

No one, to my knowledge, ever contradicted her. Customers meekly accepted their change and took their drinks.

Lil also introduced more liberal licensing laws long before they were ever passed by Parliament. It was generally possible to get a drink in the place in the early hours of most mornings at a time when the official closing time was 10pm.

The idea that the police might interfere never crossed her mind, partly because a number of the boys in blue, both on and off duty, were among her best customers. Nowadays, she would be closed down but these were more relaxed times.

Time took its toll of Lil and eventually she died but there is some doubt as to whether Lil's spirit has ever left the premises.

Staff claim that they can feel a presence in the building and footsteps are often heard moving upstairs when that area is known to be empty. Possibly the strangest incident however related to a group who were having a complementary medicine session on the premises.

Members of the group were having one-to-one massages in one of the rooms, so that there were normally only two people in the room at any time.

Strange enough, a number of people felt they were being massaged by two pairs of hands.

Perhaps the spirit of Lil still feels a need to keeps an eye on the old place and who knows, she might even be expressing her disgust about the fact that these days the Esk Hotel conforms strictly to the law.

Battle Sight

OS map, sheet 54: NO 526493

On the 2nd of January 1950, after an evening out socialising with friends in Brechin, Miss E F Smith, a local schoolteacher, was driving towards her home in Letham, a village in Angus, when her car left the road in the wintry conditions.

It was in the early hours of the morning and there were only a few scattered houses and farms on the isolated road on which she was travelling, so, rather than try to waken anyone and ask for help, Miss Smith elected to walk the rest of the way, although she was still some eight miles from her home.

As she walked along the road leading toward Dunnichen, a hamlet near Letham, she became aware of a number of flickering lights moving about in the fields about a mile away. It was only when she turned left off that road onto the road to Letham itself that she could see that the lights, which were now on her right, were in fact the flames from torches held by strangely dressed men.

Continuing towards Letham, Miss Smith found herself approximately 50 yards from the men. She could see them quite clearly, although it was so dark that she was unable to see the farm buildings behind the figures. The men were moving around what appeared to be the site of a battle, apparently trying to identify which of the dead were their comrades and which were the enemy.

What Miss Smith had apparently seen was a vision of events following the Battle of Nechtansmere, a battle that had taken place on the 20th May in the year AD685. The apparitions that Miss Smith later described were apparently Picts, members of a race who, at the time of the battle, inhabited the eastern part of what is now Scotland, north of the River Forth, just north of where the city of Edinburgh stands today.

Before the Battle of Nechtansmere, the Northumbrians, a race of people from the north of the country that would later become England, had been the dominant force in the southern Pictish territory.

The decisive victory of the Picts was of great significance as it broke the Northumbrians power and forced them to retreat to their homeland in the north of England. This removal of the foreign invaders returned the area to Pictish control and helped to lay the foundations for the emergence of the Scottish nation.

Had the Picts been defeated the whole history of Scotland would have been changed forever and it is possible that the country of Scotland might never have existed.

The location of the Battle has been argued over for years, although recent opinion favours Dunnichen. The name Nechtansmere itself has no apparent basis in local history or place names and is believed to be from an English description of the Battle. The name Dunnichen is probably derived from *Dun*, a Gaelic word for fort, and *Nechtan*, who was one of the early Pictish Kings or leaders, meaning literally 'the fort of Nechtan'.

It would therefore not be unreasonable to assume that the name Nechtansmere would itself come from the name of the Pictish leader coupled with the word mere. The use of the word mere suggests a site near a lake or pond but no sizeable stretch of water currently exists locally.

But the word mere can also mean a marsh and another possibility is that the original name of the Battle site may have been Nechtan's mire from the Scot's word mire or myre, meaning bog. An area known as The Myre exists in nearby Forfar.

Yet another Scot's word for mire is moss, and a 1794 map of the district by John Ainslie shows a moss close to Dunnichen Hill. Further research by Dr Wainwright, of the History Department at what is now Dundee University, carried out in the late 1940s, reinforced this. It is likely that the moss or mire disappeared because of agricultural improvements.

Miss Smith denied any knowledge of Dr Wainwright's work prior to her sightings although, when telling her story, she described how the Pictish warriors had walked around an invisible obstruction on the ground, presumably the now non-existent mire.

From what little is known of the Battle we do know that the Picts lured the enemy onto ground of their choosing by pretending to retreat. It would appear likely that, only when it was too late, would the Northumbrians have realised that they were caught in a trap between the Pictish fort of Nechtan and the mire.

Certainly there is further evidence of Pictish activity in the area. There are a number of Pictish stones in the nearby hamlet of Aberlemno and, in the churchyard there, stands a Pictish stone, one side of which is believed to be a pictorial representation of the Battle.

Curiously enough, had Miss Smith used the alternative road from Brechin to Letham, instead of the more direct route, she would have passed through Aberlemno within yards of this 'memorial.'

A Vivid Account

Mr James McHarg, a psychiatrist with an interest in psychic experiences, interviewed Miss Smith some twenty years after her sighting and found that, although she was then in her 70s, she was still able to describe the scenes in detail, including a full description of the clothes worn by the Picts, and of the redness of the Picts' torches. Initially, Mr McHarg had believed that Miss Smith had been referring to the flames of the torches but it had later been suggested to him that the colour might have been the red colour of the fir roots which were still used to make torches in some of the country areas as late as the 19th century.

The Statistical Account of Scotland, written in the late 18th century, when describing the Parish of Fortingall, in Perthshire, related that, 'everywhere the country people dig for the roots of fir, in the mosses, both for light and firewood'. So it is quite a logical assumption that the Picts, with the moss on their 'doorstep', had a ready supply of roots for torches.

In response to further questioning by Mr McHarg, Miss Smith explained that she had heard of the Battle, but had no idea of who had fought there.

The big question is however, did Miss Smith really see the aftermath of a Battle fought almost thirteen hundred years before? Mr McHarg's conclusion after he interviewed Miss Smith, was that, given her ability to describe the scene in such detail, she might indeed have had a genuine vision of the past.

Alternatively was Miss Smith laughing inwardly at a huge practical joke she had played on her friends, did her exertions cause her to have a particularly vivid dream when she went to bed that night, or was her vision really caused by spirits? We shall never be sure.

Considering the various types of sighting perhaps there is yet another factor we need to consider here. Namely, what Miss Smith is reputed to have seen was not the dead but the living – the survivors and their conduct in the aftermath of the battle.

There have been a number of visions of battles but these have generally been of the actual fighting. Here we have a sighting of what followed one.

Invisible Residents

Jack Dunsmuir lives at Hatton Smithy, a former blacksmith's home and workshop as the name implies, just a mile or so from the village of Inverarity in Angus.

His then second wife, a native American lady called Karen, always insisted that there were other people in the house.

Karen drew two pictures – a man who might have been the blacksmith and a woman wearing a frilled bonnet and apron.

She also described a little girl who apparently stayed next door. (The cottage was originally two separate houses.)

On a number of occasions, Karen claimed that people walked into the bedroom, bent down and did something at the fireplace before walking out again. They never ever looked at her.

She also heard footsteps coming through the house from the front door and up the stairs. One day, she was having a cup of tea with her friend when both heard someone walking upstairs.

Unremarkable, except that there are no stairs in the cottage. Years later, Jack was speaking to an elderly neighbour who asked if the stairs were still there?

This came as news to Jack who had never known of stairs and there are certainly no structural signs in the current building to indicate that it ever had stairs.

Karen also reported the front door opening and then closing without anyone coming in.

His first wife always thought that there was a presence in the property as well.

Jack himself has no perception of any presence other than one occasion when he woke up feeling a draught of cold air moving across his head and a sensation as if someone had run their hand over his head.

The family now consists of Jack, a dog, cat and two parrots. He reports that on one occasion he was awakened by the parrots making a noise despite the fact that they are normally quiet in the dark.

The cat too sometimes seems to visually follow something about the room or stare at something that Jack cannot see.

Horse Loving Ghost

One of the riding schools in Angus had not longed moved into new premises when they found that they had more than horses in and around the premises.

Although the owner did not believe in supernatural beings she soon found that in some of the buildings she got the feeling that she was not alone. Sometimes, she even thought that she caught a glimpse of a figure but quickly dismissed the idea, telling herself that she was imagining things.

One day, driving into the yard, she thought she saw her grand-daughter looking out of one of the windows at her. She thought it was odd that the little girl, who lives with her mother, was over at the yard quite so early in the morning.

Then she realised that, in any case, her grand-daughter was too small to be looking out of that particular window.

The figure was that of a young girl with blonde hair, probably aged about 11 or 12.

On another occasion however, she saw a figure crossing the school.

Later, her grand-daughter, who is aged four, told her that her sister, who she named, had been killed in a car accident.

The grand-daughter doesn't have a sister, although she sometimes talks to an invisible friend. If you ask her whom she is talking to she will tell you that it is her sister.

The buildings in the yard have been the sites of other strange happenings. A big heavy door has been seen moving of its own accord while an employee reported someone pushing past her – only – there was no one else there.

More recently, another employee was working in one of the sheds. Suddenly, there was a great crash. On investigation, it was found that a clock, which had been securely fastened to the wall, had fallen down. What was even stranger was that it was found several metres away from where it might have been expected to finish up.

Falling items seem to be quite common there. One day, the owner went into her office to find a drawing, which had been coloured in by one of the younger riders, lying on the floor behind the door. The strange thing was that the map tacks which had been used to secure it were still in the wall and the picture was not torn at all. Somehow, it had come off the wall, apparently of its own accord.

The owner's daughter was outside amongst the horses one day when she heard a 'neigh'. All of the horses were accounted for and she was certain there was no way it could have come from any of them. She was equally certain that there were no other horses around. Perhaps it was the girl's pony.

In a similar situation, she has heard a young girl's voice calling her by name. Her initial reaction was that it was her own daughter until she remembered that she was at nursery school.

Talking to a neighbour, the owner was surprised to hear that a young girl of that name and of a similar age and description to the girl she had seen had been killed in a car accident just few years before. She had a great love of ponies and it appears likely that she 'visits' the yard because of the horses.

Both grandmother and mother admit that they never believed in the supernatural before – but, after their experiences, they do now!

Glamis Castle

OS Map, sheet 54: NO 386480

Ghosts and castles go together and the castles and large houses of Angus have their fair share of ghostly inhabitants.

Glamis was not originally the site of a castle but of a hunting lodge used by the Kings of Scotland and it is thought that there may have been an earlier wooden fortification which probably stood on a mound close to the present building.

It would have made more sense strategically if the stone castle had been built on higher ground and nearby Hunter's Hill would have been a perfect location.

According to legend, attempts were made to build there. Each day, stones would be put in place and, each night, the built stones would be pulled down again.

Some sources even suggest that a voice was heard telling the builders to erect their castle down below on the boggy ground. Others say that the builders eventually realised that the Hill was inhabited by the little people who resented the intrusion.

Anyway, for one reason or another, the apparently more logical hill site was eventually abandoned and building took place on or near the present site (**10**).

Although it is often said that Malcolm II died at Glamis from wounds sustained in battle or as a result of an assassination attempt this is probably nothing more than another folk tale. Malcolm's successor, Duncan I, was killed by Macbeth during a battle fought near Elgin in 1040.

Later, Shakespeare decided to incorporate these bloody goings-on into his own version of Scottish history.

The Bard is reputed to have visited Aberdeen in 1599 so it may be that he heard of Glamis' reputation for paranormal activity and decided to

10 *Glamis Castle in the mist.*

loosely incorporate the stories into the Scottish Play. Certainly, the most famous ghost with Glamis connections is a fabrication.

The Lyon family have lived at Glamis since 1372, the year in which John Lyon, later Sir John, was granted the thaneage of Glamis by King Robert II. Four years later, Sir John married Robert's daughter, Princess Joanna, the first of many associations with the Royal family.

It was their son, also Sir John, who started work on the Castle proper, so that the original parts of the Castle are themselves monuments to over 600 years of history.

In modern times, the Castle has become best known as the childhood home of the late Queen Mother and the birthplace of Princess Margaret but, like most buildings of that vintage, the Castle is reputed to be haunted. Staff tell of three ghosts, although popular legends link Glamis to many more.

Other than the saga of Macbeth, the best known of the tales of strange happenings at Glamis is the story of the hidden room.

Late one Saturday evening, Lord Glamis was playing cards with the Earl of Crawford, who was also known as 'Tiger' and 'Earl Beardie', in one of the small rooms in the Castle. This room was situated in the walls of the crypt, which are certainly thick enough to incorporate a small chamber (**11**).

11 *The crypt at Glamis. Note the orb above the armour display mounted on the wall. The author's attempts to recreate this phenomenon failed.*

The card game continued into the night until, eventually, Saturday passed into Sunday.

There are many versions of this story but the outcome is always the same.

Some say a servant interrupted the two card players and reminded them that it was now the Sabbath whereupon Glamis is reputed to have said he would play on regardless. Other versions have Glamis or Beardie offering to gamble with 'the De'il' (Devil) himself.

Again, versions of the tale differ. Some have a tall, darkly clothed stranger arriving at the gate seeking admission to the castle while others simply have him appearing in the chamber.

One way or another, the Devil arrived to take part in the card game, after which strange noises were heard coming from the room.

The noises persisted for years until, eventually, after some 300 years, the family could put up with the strange sounds no longer and they had the room filled in and the entrance closed up. The only traces left today are the marks where 'new' stone had been added to fill up the original doorway and the view from the outside of the Castle where visitors can see the window of the room that no longer exists.

There are those who believe that Beardie still haunts the Castle having lost his soul to the Devil in the card game and certainly it is said that strange noises can still be heard coming from the room on Saturday evenings – perhaps the card game has still to be finished.

The Grey Lady

Another legend is that of the 'Grey' or 'Praying Lady', a spirit generally thought to be that of Lady Janet Douglas, the wife of the 6th Lord Glamis.

James V of Scotland was said to have had a grudge against the Douglas family or he might simply have coveted the lands and castle of the family and resolved to have them for himself. Indeed, there may have been a measure of both.

After her husband died in 1528, Lady Janet no longer had the protection of Lord Glamis and, whatever James's motives, she was taken to Edinburgh to stand trial for witchcraft.

By all accounts there was no substance to the charge. Lady Janet was reputed to have a kindly disposition but torture was reputedly used to extract a confession from her, a normal practice of the time that persisted until the witch-hunts of the 17th century.

In the face of such 'evidence' the wretched Lady Janet was found guilty and burned alive at Castle Hill in Edinburgh in 1537. Her son John was held prisoner and if he too had died the lands might well have reverted to the King.

However, it was James V who died in 1542 and eventually young John was released by an Act of the Parliament of Scotland, after which he was able to return to Glamis and claim his rightful inheritance.

Many people say they have seen the figure of a woman dressed in a grey robe, praying in the chapel (**12**), so perhaps Lady Janet also returned to Glamis to keep a motherly eye on her son and heir.

There is however, one drawback to the theory that the apparition is that of Lady Janet, the chapel had not been built at the time of her death.

Nevertheless, the tradition persists to this day that those about to enter the chapel should knock three times to warn Lady Janet of their approach.

Other stories tell of a White Lady who haunts the grounds and particularly the tree-lined avenue that leads up to the Castle. The White Lady can move much quicker than any human form and keeps pace with cars as they drive up to the Castle. Many stories are variations of others so it may be that the spectre of the white lady is in fact Lady Janet.

12 *The chapel at Glamis where Lady Janet is said to pray.*

The final ghost is that of a young page boy who was rather too mischievous for his own good.

Having got himself in to bother just once too often he was ordered to sit on a seat, a slab that jutted out from the wall of the room (**13**).

We don't know what his misdemeanour was but he was told to sit there until he was told that he could leave. Whatever happened, he was forgotten about until morning when his stiff, frozen body was discovered.

Another version of this story is that the page boy was black, while yet another suggests that he still possesses the same mischievous streak that got him into trouble in the first place. If this version is to be believed he still sits on his seat and stretches out a leg to trip the unwary.

There have also been stories that the page boy still keeps an eye on the family and he is reputed to have made a fleeting appearance at a family funeral in 1972.

13 *The stone seat where the unfortunate page boy froze to death.*

There are however many other stories which popular legend has set in Glamis and the rise of the Internet has no doubt helped the number multiply even more, so that Glamis has the reputation of being one of the most haunted places in Britain.

According to some sources, another apparition, possibly also that of Lady Janet, appears in the turret of the clock tower surrounded by flames, as if re-enacting her last moments when she was burned at the stake in Edinburgh.

The face of a young girl is reputed to appear at a window half way up one of the towers before she is pulled away. These appearances are said to be followed by the sound of knocking and banging.

One particularly macabre account suggests that a young woman runs through the grounds with her hand up to her bleeding mouth. The inference is that her tongue had been cut out to ensure her silence about some dastardly deed.

Another version of this story describes the woman as having her tongue cut out and her hands cut off to ensure her silence after she discovered a closely guarded family secret.

Yet another ghost said to frequent the grounds is known for obvious reasons as Jack the Runner, an extremely gaunt man who can be seen running at speed through the Castle precincts. According to legend, Jack was hung for some misdemeanour, although again, no one really knows.

Inside the Castle itself, some people are reputed to have seen a tall, bearded clansman, who stalks the corridors before eventually disappearing through solid walls. There are also tales of foes coming to the Castle and being bricked up in the walls and left to starve to death, so it might be that the highlander is one of the soldiers who met that dreadful fate.

Alternatively, if indeed Beardie's ghost roams the Castle, it might be that the bearded figure is not a highlander but the gambler, looking for someone to join him and the Devil in their unfinished card game.

A butler on the Castle staff is said to have hung himself and he is reported to re-appear in the room where the gruesome deed took place, while there are also stories of another ghost appearing on the roof of the Castle.

If some of the stories are to be believed, guests in the Castle sometimes have rude awakening. There are tales of visitors having their bed covers pulled off them by unseen forces and a ghost, dressed in armour, is reputed to visit the rooms of an evening, checking on the sleeping guests.

One visitor is said to have awakened in the early hours of the morning and heard the sound of hammering. The suggestion is that the sound is of the scaffold being built for Lady Janet, except, of course, the poor woman was burnt, not hanged.

Before radio, television and the Internet, people had to find ways to amuse themselves and storytelling was one way of passing the long winter nights. Many of these tales probably have their roots in the oral tradition and, with each telling, the stories have probably been embellished and exaggerated.

On the other hand, would you like to spend the night alone in the Castle?

For details visit the website <www.glamis-castle.co.uk> or telephone 01307 840393.

The Trial and Execution of Margaret Wishart

Arbroath woman, Margaret Wishart, was tried and convicted at Forfar of the murder of her sister Jean in 1827.

The charges were that on several dates in October the previous year she administered a quantity of arsenic, mixed in porridge or gruel, to her sister and her sister's newly born child, whereby Jean died on the 8th October and the baby the following day.

A contemporary account described Margaret as a tidy and smart girl who was in the service of Provost Webster of Forfar for some five or six years.

She had three sisters, two of whom were older than her and married, and the third, Jean, who had been blind from birth. Jean lived in Applegate in Arbroath with the girls' widowed mother.

Margaret had a 'young man', Andrew Roy, who regularly visited her in Forfar but did not appear to be in any rush to make an 'honest woman' of her.

It was when her mother died and there was no one else to look after Jean that Margaret took a house in Orchard Street in Arbroath. There, she made a meagre living from having four lodgers, one of whom was Andrew Roy, and by occasionally taking in washing.

Some eighteen months after she started her new venture her life suddenly changed.

Andrew Roy was well thought off in the town. As a regular churchgoer and a fine tradesman with his own business he appeared to be an upright citizen.

Yet, whatever Margaret's understanding of their relationship might have been, Andrew obviously had other ideas and in September 1826 he sold up and apparently left for America.

Whether this might have raised suspicions of some sort in Margaret's mind is not clear but if she had any such fears they were confirmed at the beginning of October. Margaret could see that Jean was ill and she sent for the midwife who confirmed that Jean was expecting a child.

Jean refused to name the father and, although there was no evidence that the handsome Andrew Roy was the culprit, it is likely that Margaret may have harboured such suspicions in view of his sudden departure.

Within days, Jean was delivered of a male child but both mother and baby were soon gravely ill and died within hours of each other.

Foul Play Suspected

Initially, there was no suggestion of foul play and Jean and her son were buried in the cemetery at St Vigeans.

Before long however, some of the neighbours, namely Catherine and Mary Greig and Bell Sands, were openly saying that Jean Wishart had been poisoned.

Inevitably, this came to the attention of the authorities who decided that the matter was worthy of investigation.

As a result, the decision was taken to exhume the bodies which, for some odd reason, was carried out one Sunday during morning worship.

If the idea was that the local people would be too busy to notice it backfired badly.

The congregation could hear the sounds of digging and, ignoring the preacher, they were soon all on their feet, looking out of the windows at the strange sight of bodies being dug up.

Samples from the stomachs and intestines of both bodies were taken and sent off for examination. That evening, a local doctor, Dr Arrott, confirmed that he had found traces of arsenic in the stomach of the woman although he had found nothing suspicious in the body of the child.

On the Monday morning, statements were taken from the neighbours and Margaret Wishart was arrested and brought before the sheriff at Arbroath. She was detained in the Tolbooth to await further instructions from Crown Counsel.

If the almost public nature of the exhumation had started the local rumour mill then Margaret's detention provided more ammunition for the gossips.

Despite the fact that Margaret Wishart was generally known as a decent but poor young woman, the poisoning of her blind sister, the illegitimate child and the sudden disappearance of Andrew Roy all resulted in wild speculation. Needless to say, there were many know-alls who 'werna not at a' surprised; they aye thocht there was something wrang an that it was easy seen that Jean Wishart an Andrew Roy were ower thrang' (intimately associated).

On Trial

The trial opened in Perth on 12th April 1827. Unfortunately for Margaret Wishart the evidence against her, although largely circumstantial, was fairly damning in the eyes of the jury.

Various witnesses testified that they saw Margaret feeding the deceased but didn't see her taking any of the food herself.

Similarly, the court heard that Margaret had been unwilling to send for a doctor, objecting that a doctor would be able to do little and, on another occasion, on the grounds, common enough at the time, of expense.

On Margaret's behalf, witnesses, who unfortunately were easily dismissed due to their own criminal connections, testified that Jean had gone to purchase poison herself.

What did come out in evidence was that Jean already had a three-year-old child and that both children were Andrew Roy's. There were suggestions too from witnesses that the deceased had previously claimed that both Margaret and Andrew Roy had 'bad-used' her.

At first sight it is difficult to ignore the evidence that Jean Wishart's stomach contained traces of arsenic. If it was not given to her by her sister it could only have been self-administered. Did Jean Wishart want to end it all – it seems unlikely.

But, and it is a huge but, although it was possible to test for the presence of arsenic at the time it was not until 1836 that an indisputable scientific test was devised. Coupled with the fact that the symptoms exhibited by the deceased could also have been due to a ruptured gastric ulcer means there is reasonable doubt as to whether Jean was murdered and so whether the luckless Margaret was guilty of anything.

The Jury Decides

The jury were less charitable. After the closing speeches they took just half an hour to find Margaret Wishart 'guilty' of the murder of her sister while the charge of murdering the child was found 'not proven'.

Having been found guilty, Margaret Wishart was sentenced to death and she was transferred to Forfar where the sentence was to be carried out. Ironically, the death warrant was sent to Provost Webster, Margaret's former employer, who had the unpleasant duty of reading it out to a meeting of the Town Council on 28th April.

The Provost advised that many people were convinced of Margaret's innocence and he felt that the evidence against her was entirely circumstantial. A petition seeking mercy had already been sent to the King from the authorities in Perth and he proposed that the Forfar Town Council should follow suit. His recommendation was unanimously agreed.

Clemency was not recommended and there was to be no stay of execution although in the end, due to Margaret Wishart's mental state, the execution was delayed until the 16th June. Unsurprisingly, Forfar had no hangman and Thomas Williams, the Edinburgh hangman, agreed to carry out the deed for a fee of ten guineas (£10.50) plus three guineas (£3.15) for his travelling expenses.

On a sunny Saturday afternoon, thousands gathered to see the final act of this long running tragedy. At thirteen minutes after three o'clock Margaret Wishart signalled her readiness and within minutes it was all over.

As was the custom of the time, the body was conveyed to the Professor of Anatomy at Edinburgh University to be used for anatomical research.

Another Suspect

The account of Margaret Webster's trial and execution is taken from *Tales and Legends of Forfarshire* by Alexander Lowson. Mr Lowson was convinced of Margaret's innocence and he introduced another possible culprit.

Although he did not see the man himself he felt that from the description given to him, he was Andrew Roy.

The owner of the alehouse in the Osnaburg pend (**14**), a Mrs Petrie, said there was something 'no usual' about the man who frequented her establishment on the day before the execution. He would speak only to order his drink and then sit for no longer than five minutes at a time, always appearing to be 'restless and nervous'.

The stranger would appear from different directions but, according to Lowson's account, 'the spot on which they were erecting the gibbet might be compared to the candle round which this human moth was flickering'.

Some three weeks after the hanging, some boys fishing on Forfar Loch spotted what they thought at first was a bundle of old clothes. Pulling the bundle to the shore they were horrified to find that it was a body, so badly decomposed as to be unrecognisable.

No identification was ever made and the body was laid to rest. Mr Lowson remained convinced that the corpse was Andrew Roy, whom he described as 'the arch-fiend and prime mover' in the tragedy that ended the lives of both Jean and Margaret Wishart.

14 *Osnaburg Street with the pend at the far end.*

That was not the end of the matter as a tract written shortly afterwards explained:

> In the house formerly occupied by her [Margaret Wishart] in Arbroath, there is occasionally heard (particularly in the night time), a fearful noise, as if of tongues, doors rattling, fire-irons clattering, &c.; so that the present occupants lose many an hour and night's sleep. Mr. William Prophet; stoneware merchant, and family, occupy the whole house. Several people who have had occasion to be in the house, have heard the noises, and concur with the family in speaking of them. Whatever the cause of them may be, the truth of this statement is beyond all controversy. Ghost or no ghost, the family are fearfully annoyed.

Unfortunately, there is no clue as to whom the spectre might be or even whether it is male or female. Is it the unfortunate victim, blind Jean, the alleged culprit, Margaret, or perhaps even the dastardly Andrew Roy? There is no way of knowing.

Today, Orchard Street has no houses on it, running as it does between a supermarket and the railway line, so there is no one about to report mysterious noises or ghostly figures – unless someone out there knows differently!

Forfar's Witches

The burgh of Forfar is the nearest town to Glamis but it is probably better known for its witches than for ghost sightings.

Although there were witches in other Angus towns, Forfar was where witch hunting was most avidly prosecuted. So much so, that, for a period of almost two years from 1661, the Town Council, spurred on by an enthusiastic Kirk minister, actively sought out witches and put them on trial.

The accused were generally women of low status, often the most powerless in their society. Sometimes, they suffered from some form of disability which made them look or act differently from their fellows which was enough to mark them out as being witches. Others were simply herbalists who had treated someone who later died or perhaps they had crossed a more powerful figure.

At the time, it was believed that witches could be identified by strange marks on their bodies or the fact that they did not bleed or feel any pain if pricked with a pin.

Such beliefs led to the rise of witchfinders, men who claimed that they could identify witches by those means. The financial rewards for identifying witches was considerable, so that the witchfinders made a better living the more witches they exposed.

One of the best known witchfinders was John Kincaid, a native of Tranent. He proved so successful in Forfar that he was made a freeman of the Burgh, although he was later exposed as a fraud and imprisoned. He was eventually released because of his extreme age but only after giving an undertaking that he would cease his deceitful activities.

Once a woman had been identified she was normally interrogated which generally involved torture of one sort or another. Apart from purely physical methods such as the branks, a form of face mask that kept the victim from sleeping or drinking and, probably most important from an interrogator's point of view, putting the curse of the Devil on him, the accused was also often deprived of sleep, a technique which causes hallucinations which may be responsible for some of the more lurid confessions.

Once found guilty, which was generally the fate of these unfortunate women, they were put to death by first being strangled and then burned in a barrel containing tar.

The principal player in the Forfar drama was one Helen Guthrie who named some 28 witches out of over 40 suspects. Most were executed although some were only, if that is the correct word in the circumstances, banished from the parish, for that too, may have amounted in many instances to an effective death sentence

It is not clear what Helen's motives were. Her daughter, Janet, had also been accused of witchcraft, probably thought guilty by association. Whether Helen hoped to deflect attention away from her daughter or whether she had some other agenda it failed to save her from execution, although Janet survived.

Eventually, as so often happens, it was realised that the situation was both farcical and out of control and the whole sorry episode was brought to an end.

The story of the witches is well-known today and apparently, as we shall shortly see, a coven still 'meets' in one of the local hostelries.

Lost In The Loch

We have already seen that the story of King Malcolm II of Scotland staying at Glamis in 1034 is thought to be simply a legend, although the story persists along with the 'account' of his assassination.

In those days, being the King meant that you had many enemies and even members of the monarch's own family often had designs on getting the crown for themselves.

The list of potential suspects is therefore a long one but legend has it that as Malcolm slept at Glamis one night a group of armed men entered the castle and murdered him before making their escape by riding off towards Forfar.

It had been a particularly hard winter and the Loch, which was then much larger and deeper than it is now, had frozen over to such a depth that it was capable of bearing the weight of men on horses and even horses and carts.

Unfortunately for the assassins, spring had arrived and the ice had started to melt.

In the darkness, men and horses, intent on making their escape from the murder scene as quickly as possible, galloped on to the thawing surface. The ice was no longer strong enough to bear such a weight and they disappeared into the icy water and drowned.

Their screams of terror were heard in the town and when daylight came the locals searched for the bodies. No trace of the murderers was ever found and although pieces of armour have been dredged from the Loch these are generally reckoned to be from a later period.

It is said however, that on certain nights, the ghosts of the men can be seen, visible only from the waist up, trying vainly to escape from the clutches of the icy waters.

As so often happens, there is another version of this tale. Although the basic details are similar, King Malcolm is said to have been out riding at Thornton Wood on Hunter Hill, the place where Glamis Castle might have been built but for the intervention of the little people.

There, he was set upon and murdered by three armed men who attempted to escape across the Loch with the same outcome as previously described.

According to this account, it was believed that the Thane of Glamis was involved because he constantly visited the crime scene.

Much later, he was visited by his neighbour, the Thane of Angus, and his beautiful daughter Finella.

Glamis apparently took a shine to the young lady and, while out walking in a nearby wood, he asked her to marry him. He is then said to have called upon the spirit of the dead King to witness their betrothal.

Malcolm, apparently appeared, dressed in his shroud, much to the young woman's horror. To make matters worse, the spectre obviously blamed Glamis for his death and gestured threateningly to him before disappearing.

Needless to say, the ghost had his revenge. The couple went on to have three sons, each of whom died violently. One was drowned, another was pushed off the castle battlements by an unseen force and the other was gored to death by a mysterious stag.

Even then, the spectre was not finished with the family as Glamis and his wife did not escape unscathed either. In two separate incidents, each was found strangled close to the spot where the ghost of Malcolm had appeared in response to Glamis' bizarre request.

The figure of a young woman is also said to appear near the Loch. According to legend, she had been unfaithful to her lover and she was buried alive as a punishment while her unfortunate suitor was so devastated that he committed suicide.

Spirits in the Pub

Osnaburg is the name of a coarse woven cloth which was originally produced in the town of Osnabruck in Germany. Its commercial potential quickly became apparent to the merchants and manufacturers of Forfar and the cloth became one of the staple products woven there.

The name was also taken up as a street name and Osnaburg Street, built in 1783, was probably a weavers' settlement.

Osnaburg Street can be accessed through a small pend, an arched passageway, which connects it to the High Street. It has already been mentioned as the site of the alehouse where the narrator of the tale of Jean Wishart first became aware of the strange man whom he believed had some connection with her murder; the man he believed to be Andrew Roy, the father of Jean's children and a possible suspect if she was indeed murdered.

Whether it is on the same spot as the alehouse or not, Osnaburg Street today still boasts a public house called, unsurprisingly, the Osnaburg Bar (**15**).

There is no suggestion that the ghost of Jean Wishart stalks the Bar but it has been the site of a number of unexplained incidents

Various spirits of the non-alcoholic variety have been detected and there appear to be

15 *The Osnaburg Bar harbours a number of spirits.*

83

presences in both the bar and the flat above. One is thought to be a chimney sweep, or at least a young boy who would have been sent up the chimney. Why he died, whether as a result of an accident or of natural causes, is not clear.

There may also be a spirit of another youngster present, but again, the cause of death is not clear although it might be that he/she was murdered. (This may be the young chimney sweep.)

In recent years, staff and customers in the Osnaburg have certainly experienced some strange sights and sounds.

A woman serving coffee was not too alarmed when she saw a shadow in the lounge area. It was only when she noticed it moving that she became frightened as she knew there was no one through there. The colour drained from her face prompting others to ask if she had seen a ghost? Of course she had!

There also appears to be a presence in the cellar and some members of staff are unwilling to go down there on their own.

As a result of the supernatural activity, the Osnaburg Bar has become a focus for paranormal researchers in recent years and, recently, the site was visited by a team of paranormal investigators, including a psychic who found three 'new' spirits.

In the public bar the medium felt the presence of a nanny and possibly young children.

Through in the lounge he felt the presence of a coven of witches, although such an experience would come as no great surprise in Forfar with its turbulent experience of witch hunts in the 17th century.

The medium also felt there was a young woman connected to the house nearest the pend.

He also detected another presence whom he was able to describe in great detail. In fact, his description was so accurate that the staff present knew immediately that he was referring to Harry Kettles, a regular in the bar who died recently. Harry was apparently a man of strong opinions who loved to debate issues with fellow customers. When the writer visited the pub to inquire about the other spirits the barman was quick to point to the small plaque, in Harry's memory, which is attached to one of the pillars.

Two of the local Masonic Lodges, Lour and Kilwinning, met at one time in the property above the pub and during one of the ceremonies one of the brethren died. Afterwards, his colleagues believed they could feel his presence and it was decided to carry out the ceremony again, an act which appeared to release his spirit.

Although the tale is well known, no formal record of the occasion exists. The most popular theory is that he was a tyler, an official responsible for keeping out non-members, who died while setting out chairs for a meeting or putting them away afterwards.

Even More Spirits

Forfar is blessed with many licensed premises and quite a number seem to have attracted spirits of the supernatural variety over the years.

During the 1980s there were strange happenings at the Queen's Hotel. At one time the pub on the ground floor and the publican's accommodation upstairs had been linked by a bell to allow simple communication between the two areas.

By that time however the flat was unoccupied so one can imagine the consternation when the bell started ringing one Wednesday evening.

There was no obvious explanation and the circumstances were mysterious enough to reduce the customers in the bar to silence, no mean feat in a busy pub.

A similar incident occurred a few weeks later and the problem was only resolved when the bell was removed for good.

The Royal Hotel in Castle Street is also thought to be haunted. Footsteps are regularly heard, doors slam and telephones ring in empty rooms. Some of the strange happenings there are thought to be linked to the suicide of a maid servant in the old stables during the early part of the 20th century.

These are not the only hotels with strange stories. Over at the Stag Hotel it is believed that there may be a poltergeist in residence as beer barrels, tables and chairs are regularly overturned, with no logical explanation as to why this should happen.

One former owner had two large Alsatian dogs but even they would not enter certain parts of the building.

Forfar appears to be a regular haunt, as it were, of strange, unexplained phenomena. At one stage, passers-by walking along the street could see ladies in Victorian costumes standing at the windows of the dental practice in East High Street.

There have been strange occurrences too at the local branch of the British Legion where, in the small bar, one of the regulars apparently continued to visit his favourite hostelry, despite the fact he had died a few weeks before.

In a house on the Dundee Loan a young boy was particularly distressed to waken up to find an old man in bed beside him. The old man suddenly disappeared.

There is a similar tale about a joiner at Lunanhead. He went to bed one night with his brother. They awoke to find they were also sharing their bed with an old man. One of them apparently punched the old man who again, disappeared.

A man who regularly walked the area with his wife always assured her that if he died before her he would return to the spot to meet her.

As she sat on a bench after his death a butterfly flew down and landed on her leg. A chance occurrence or the fulfilment of a promise to a loved one, who can say?

Perhaps the most bizarre tale of all concerned a local photographer who took a number of pictures at a social gathering. This was in the days when cameras still used films and it was only once the pictures were developed that someone noticed that one of them showed a gentleman who appeared to have a logo, similar to the head of a cavalier, on his shirt.

The situation was not as simple as it first appeared however as the man had no logo on his shirt.

The negative was sent to the company that had produced the film but they could give no logical explanation for the 'head'. Similarly, the negative was examined by Glasgow CID but they couldn't solve the mystery either.

Because of the existence of Hadrian's and the Antonine Wall, people often assume that the Romans were kept south of Strathmore by the fiercesome tribes that lived north of the Forth-Clyde valley during the time of the Roman occupation.

Of course, this is far from the truth. The Romans invaded lowland Scotland on three occasions so that Angus had its share of Roman visitors and, thanks to the use of aerial photography, we can now identify several Roman sites within the county.

There was a Roman fort at Stracathro and another at Inverquharity, just north of Kirriemuir, both of which are thought to have been used in the campaigns of Agricola during the first century AD.

The Inverquharity fort was situated where the South Esk meets the River Prosen on what was later the site of Inverquharity Castle, of which we shall hear more later, proving that it occupied a fine strategic position.

Further north, the fort at Stracathro occupied another historical site, although this time the replacement building, Stracathro Church and graveyard, still exists. Some accounts claim that John Balliol, the King of Scots, surrendered his throne to Edward I of England there in 1296.

Aerial photography has also identified a supply camp, which probably supplied the Stracathro fort, on part of what is now Gilrivie Farm on the shores of the Montrose Basin and there were also a number of camps along the banks of the South Esk, close to the fort itself.

With considerable Roman activity in the area over a period of time it is not surprising that one young woman who worked as a Saturday girl in the former Woolworth's store in Forfar says that the older employees claimed that Roman soldiers were seen regularly, apparently marching through the store. The figures were seen only from the knees up, suggesting that the original road they walked on was lower than the present floor level.

Sightings of phantom armies have been numerous throughout Scotland and in the mid 17th century a force of armed men were seen hovering just above the ground over the moor of Forfar.

Restenneth Priory

Just a few miles east of Forfar, on the A932 road to Montrose, lies Restenneth Priory (**16**).

Restenneth, which is one of the earliest surviving stone buildings in Scotland, is thought to have been founded by Nechtan, King of the Picts, probably sometime around 715, although, in common with many other old sacred buildings, the Priory may have been built on a site which had pagan origins.

(This particular Nechtan was a descendant of the earlier King Nechtan who gave his name to the battlefield of Dunnichen, or Nechtansmere if you prefer, where Miss Smith saw the aftermath of the battle.)

The Priory was later granted a charter by David I (c.1084–1153), who gifted various lands to it. David was succeeded by his grandson Malcolm IV who gave Restenneth to Jedburgh Abbey and it was then that it became a religious house used by the Augustinian Order.

Restenneth was subsequently extended while occupied by members of the Order, although later, during the Wars of Independence, much of the building was destroyed.

In later years, many of the Priory's rights and privileges were restored and it is reputedly the resting place of Robert the Bruce's son, Prince John, the only member of the family not interred in Dunfermline Abbey.

For a time, Restenneth also served as the parish church for the burgh of Forfar itself but this role ceased soon after the Reformation.

Restenneth then withered in importance and passed through the hands of various landowners before being rescued from use as a shelter for cattle when it came under the protection of the relevant historical body in 1919.

Today, it has as one of its neighbours, Angus Archives, surely a suitable use for a place of heritage.

The Augustinian Order based at Restenneth may have been known as the White Friars, due to the colour of their habits. In medieval times however, it seems unlikely that their robes would have stayed clean for long and it is that fact which makes the following tale so intriguing.

16 *Restenneth Priory; the spirits don't welcome lone women.*

The Priory is regularly visited by individuals and parties interested in its history. One group included a small boy who wandered off and was missing for a time.

When he was eventually found he explained that he had been speaking to 'the man in the brown dressing gown'. It seems an obvious description of one of the men who would have resided at Restenneth.

Restenneth can also be less than welcoming to individual women. Several, exploring the ruins on their own, have complained of a strange, cold, feeling, as if they were not welcome there. Of course, there would have been no women allowed in a male only order so it may be that women are still not appreciated by the spirits who 'inhabit' this old religious site.

Other stories suggest at least one female friendly friar among the abbots and monks who make regular appearances in the caretaker's house at the Priory. At least one apparition has lost his head but another is said to tip his hat to lady visitors. You certainly find a better class of ghost at Restenneth.

Restenneth is open to the public during daylight hours.

Jock Barefut

Earl Beardie, as well as being willing to play cards with the Devil, was an exceptionally cruel individual, although he lived in times when barbaric acts were common.

He is reputed to have hanged a number of unfortunates who had displeased him, including a wandering minstrel who angered him with his forecasts, from the metal hooks in the south-east wall of Finavon Castle.

As the minstrel wandered through the grounds of the castle his singing was overheard by Lady Crawford who was so taken with his performance that she conducted him into the presence of her husband. The minstrel's song, which foretold of the death of Beardie's ally Earl Douglas and his own eventual defeat in battle, angered him so much that he had the unfortunate player hanged from one of the hooks.

Beardie had a favourite tree, a Spanish chestnut that grew in the courtyard of the Castle. Even then, the tree was ancient, as it had, according to legend, grown from a chestnut dropped by a Roman soldier.

The tree was one of the largest in the Kingdom and was renowned for the beauty of its grain which was such that many items of furniture and items, such as snuff boxes, were said to have been made from its wood.

It was under this tree, known as the covin tree, that the Earls met their guests or drank a stirrup cup prior to departure. A covin tree was where Scottish aristocracy greeted and took their leave of their guests. More sinisterly perhaps, a covin tree was also 'the tree of punishment or many hangings' and Beardie used the tree on occasions rather than the metal hooks.

It is said that one day, a messenger or ghillie known as Jock, a lad of about 16 years of age, was on his way from Careston to Finhaven, presumably without any shoes or other coverings on his feet, when he cut a stick from the tree, an action which angered Beardie so much that he had the unfortunate youth hanged from the tree.

The incident gave rise to a rhyme:

> Earl Beardie ne'er will dee
> Nor puir Jock Barefoot be set free
> As lang's there grows a chestnut tree.

Legend has it that the tree then proceeded to wither and die, although according to the 19th-century Angus historian, Andrew Jervise, it survived until about 1740 when a series of severe frosts killed it.

To this day, the spirit of Jock Barefut, barefooted and bareheaded, apparently wanders the road between Careston and Finavon. Despite his cruel end, he is reputed to be a Puck like spirit, always looking to play tricks on innocent travellers.

According to Jervise, 'His freaks are curious, and withal inoffensive, and, on reaching a certain burn on the road vanishes from view in a blaze of fire!'

There are also tales of a White Lady who is said to visit the same district but details are sparse and little is known of this particular spirit.

Cortachy Castle   OS Map, sheet 54: NO 396596

Cortachy Castle, situated a few miles north of Kirriemuir, is home to the Ogilvy family, the Earls of Airlie, and is reputedly haunted by a ghostly drummer.

There are a number of versions of the story, although the outcome is the same. The best known tale is that the then Earl believed that the drummer was having an affair with his wife although others suggest that the drummer failed to beat his drum to warn of the approach of an enemy force or actually betrayed the Earl by siding with one of his enemies.

For whatever reason, the Earl flung the drummer and his drum from the battlements of the castle in a fit of rage and some accounts even suggest that the drummer was forced inside his drum before the dreadful act took place.

Before his death, the drummer placed a curse on the family and it is said that whenever the drum is heard it signifies the death of one of the family.

Another version suggests that it is not just the sound of the drummer that warns of the death of a member of the Airlie family and one tale, describing an incident that took place in 1845, mentions the sound of fifes, small flute style pipes, being played.

Early in the year 1845, Miss Margaret Dalrymple went to spend time at Cortachy as guests of the Earl and his wife. The storyteller, Mrs Ann Day, had accompanied her, probably acting as her chaperone.

They arrived late in the evening and, as Miss Dalrymple rested before dinner, she became aware of the sound of fifes followed by the beating of a drum. She described the sound as if coming from beneath the floor.

At dinner, she remarked on the music, whereupon Lord Airlie dropped his knife and fork and left the room without saying a word.

The following day, Mrs Day was alone in Miss Dalrymple's room when she heard the sound of a carriage driving up and then stopping, followed by the sound of a second carriage arriving and stopping. After the second carriage halted, she heard the sound of marching feet, as if a troop of soldiers were nearby.

This sound was then followed by the sound of fifes which she could hear so clearly that she half expected to find the piper in the room.

Finally, she heard the beating of a drum, which she later described as being 'something indescribably disagreeable & as if the drummer were making his way through the floor'.

There was no obvious source of the sounds.

Some months later, the Countess of Airlie died giving birth to twins, although whether this can be realistically attributed to the curse is open to debate.

Although the two ladies later shared their experiences, neither had been aware of the apparent significance of the music initially and when Miss Dalrymple had first mentioned it at dinner another guest had taken her aside and discreetly explained the situation to her.

A similar tale was told by another lady of the highest character, identified only as Miss S. She too had been a visitor at the castle on another occasion. The then Lord Airlie had been afflicted by gout but his ailment was described as slight.

As the lady was out walking in the woods close to the castle she became aware of bagpipes being played so clearly that she thought that perhaps some form of ceremony was being held in a nearby village.

Although initially the sound was all around her it suddenly became much more distinct and she was able to follow it back to the castle where it stopped as she reached the chapel door. At no point could she could see any possible source of the music.

Miss S started to relate her story at dinner but quickly realised that it was not well received. Again, another dinner guest later explained the significance of what she had heard.

Within days, Lord Airlie's condition deteriorated and he became seriously ill and died. The curse of the drummer had struck again.

Airlie Castle
OS Map, sheet 53: NO 295521

The Ogilvy family seem to attract the harbingers of death type of spirit as the other Ogilvy seat at Airlie Castle also has its own phantom in the form of a ram. The ram, known as the 'doom of Airlie', is said to circle the castle when some catastrophe is about to take place or a family member is about to die.

John of Inverquharity
OS Map, sheet 54: NO 411579

Many of the tales of folklore and legend of Angus were collected by Alexander Lowson. This one, which, like the story from Chaucer, could be titled the Priest's Tale, came into Lowson's hands by a stroke of luck.

He was having his picnic lunch among the ruins of the Castle of Inverquharity when he spotted a dove being chased by a hawk. The dove disappeared from sight and, having lost its prey, the hawk flew off.

Suddenly, the dove came tumbling out of the old ruined chimney close to where Lowson was sitting. With it fell an old leather pouch, like the pencil cases in which the scholars of old kept their pens and slate pencils.

After comforting and then releasing the dove, he turned his attention to the pencil case. Inside, were several sheets of parchment, each covered with neat well-formed writing, while the initial letter of each paragraph had been painted in bright colours like an illuminated manuscript.

The writing was in Medieval Latin and Lowson had to get the local minister to translate it for him. The dreadful story it told is related below.

Sir John Ogilvy was known throughout the district as a cruel heartless man. Probably because the old priest had been a close friend of the Laird's father, Sir John showed him a measure of courtesy that he extended to no one else.

The miller on the estate was John White, who had a fine looking wife although she was middle aged, and an extremely beautiful daughter called Lily.

The result was that Sir John visited the mill oftener than was strictly necessary although the miller, flattered by the Laird's attention, failed to see anything sinister in the situation.

At some point, Lady Ogilvy was with child and the miller's wife was sent for to nurse her. Again, the miller believed that this was the measure of the Laird's affection for his family.

The miller's wife was needed at the castle for a number of weeks. One Saturday night, as the priest was preparing for the following day's service, he was visited by the wife who was now due to return home.

She went on to confess that she had sinned with Sir John. The old priest was very angry, knowing that the unfortunate woman would have had no option but to give in to the Laird's demands.

He prayed almost as if he had been possessed, asking for a sign showing that either forgiveness would be granted or to be shown that the Laird's conduct would be followed by a curse.

As he lay in front of the altar, an angel appeared who told him;

> The God of Heaven has heard your prayer,
> He loves your zeal and verity
> Today, you'll from your holy chair
> Curse John of Inverquharity
> The poor he's starved and whipped and killed,
> His cup of wrong is almost filled,

The God of Heaven he's sore offended,
His lease of life is nearly ended

The hoolet [owl] shall croak on his castle roof hie,
The hare on his hearthstone soundly sleep,
The lark and the mavis shall sing with glee
When they carry him dead to his castle Keep.

His spirit for ages shall find no repose,
But shall wander and shriek where he ruined the maid
Whom he scourged and hanged and foully betrayed.

The priest came round to realise that he had been lying beside the altar for hours. Despite that, every word he had heard was burnt in his brain and he knew exactly what he had been charged to do.

There was large turnout for the service, including Sir John and Lady Ogilvy. The priest found himself getting bogged down by the emotion of the situation but eventually he found his voice, loudly cursing the member of the congregation who had been guilty of the heinous crime of adultery.

He announced, just as he had been told, that the sinner's home would become the habitation of the owl and the hare, while his dwelling would be cursed and become the haunt of evil spirits. Life would be so horrendous that his descendants would feel unable to stay there and the lands would pass to strangers. Finally, he prophesied that the wicked one would die a sudden and unnatural death.

All eyes were on Sir John although he remained unmoved by the old priest's outburst but from that day, until the day of his death however, he never spoke another word to the old priest.

Probably realising that the miller's wife had been the source of the priest's information, he took his revenge against the luckless John White instead.

Revenge

A trumped up charge of killing one of his deer, a hanging offence, was laid against the miller. White produced several witnesses to state that he couldn't have been the culprit but with Sir John both judge and jury in his own court the miller was sentenced to hang and until the execution could be carried out he was locked away in the lowest dungeon.

Against the advice of her mother, Lily White went to plead with the Laird for her father's life. Hearing her desperate pleas, Sir John agreed to spare the miller if she would share his bed. Lily agonised before finally agreeing to submit herself to the Laird.

After having his prize however, Sir John immediately went back on his word. Even more cruelly, he forced Lily to watch as her father was hung from a tree near the castle.

The result of the trauma was that Lily had a severe mental breakdown. Finding her wandering aimlessly, the old priest took her to her home, only to find that the poor girl's mother had hanged herself.

Some three weeks after her father's death, Lily was found drowned. In her deluded state, she had tried to cross to a small island to pick flowers.

All the while, Sir John was enjoying life as normal. Just two months after the miller had been hanged there was big hunting party at the castle. The hunters had had a good day and Sir John himself had speared a massive wild boar. As they rode back to the castle everyone was in good spirits and looking forward to an enjoyable dinner and some entertainment after their day's sport.

Suddenly, Sir John's horse stumbled and he was thrown. His head hit a rock with such force that his neck was broken and his servants covered his body in a white sheet, leaving only his face uncovered.

As they passed the tree where the miller had been hung, the evil Laird's eyes suddenly shot out from his head and his blackened tongue lolled from his mouth.

As was customary at the time, the body was watched until it could be buried. The custom, known as lykewake, was meant to guard the corpse against the evil spirits working for the Devil who would try to snatch the soul of the deceased before it could be given a proper Christian burial.

Unsurprisingly, in Sir John's case the custom failed miserably. His body was surrounded by 24 candles that would suddenly go out without warning while the room would fill with evil spirits that sat on the body and hissed and spat on it.

For years after, the country people insisted that the castle was haunted every night by the ghost of the dead Laird.

Just as the angel had prophesied, it was impossible to live in the castle and the family had to abandon it. Today it is a ruin, no doubt still inhabited by the owl and the hare.

The Haunted Museums of Angus

The building that houses the Signal Tower Museum in Arbroath has an interesting history in itself having served as the home base for the off-duty keepers from the Bell Rock lighthouse and their families (**17**). Most readers will be aware of the story of the Bell Rock described in Robert Southey's epic poem, The Inchcape Rock.

The Inchcape or Bell Rock, which is situated some twelve miles east of Arbroath, has long been a danger to shipping and the poem relates how the Abbot of Aberbrothock had placed a bell on the Rock to warn mariners of the danger.

17 *The Signal Tower museum; the ghost checked out a new curator.*

Sir Ralph the Rover, a well-known pirate, cut the bell from the Rock and was later drowned when his own ship foundered on it.

The Rock continued to be a danger to shipping over the centuries and, in the early 1800s, the Commissioners for Northern Lighthouses decided to build a lighthouse on it to warn shipping of the hazard.

They engaged Robert Stevenson, a member of the well-known lighthouse building family, to design and supervise the building of the lighthouse.

The work was carried out between 1807 and 1811 and the Bell Rock light was formally lit on the first of February of the latter year.

The lighthouse keepers served on the Bell Rock for a period of six weeks at a time and then spent two weeks ashore. There were four keepers in total and one was changed every two weeks although, if there was bad weather and the relief boat was unable to reach the lighthouse on four successive days, the keeper due to be taken off had to serve for another six weeks!

Stevenson was also responsible for the design and building of the Regency style Signal Tower which was the shore station which housed the relief lighthouse keepers and their families from 1813 until the mid 1950s.

The Signal Tower takes its name from its other function which was to be part of a simple method of communicating between the shore and the lighthouse in the days before electronic means.

The strange device on top of the Tower served that very purpose. Mounted on the pole on top of the building is a 14" (35cm) diameter ball and there is a similar piece of apparatus on the Lighthouse itself.

It was one of the duties of the keeper at the Signal Tower to look at the Lighthouse through his telescope every morning at 9am to see if the ball on the Rock had been raised. If it had been he would know that all was well and he would raise the onshore ball to acknowledge the signal.

If however, the ball on the Lighthouse was not raised he then had to travel to the Rock to find out what the problem was.

On occasions, the Signal Tower's pole was used for other signals. If one of the wives gave birth while her husband was on duty on the Rock he would be given news of the birth by a novel method. If the baby was a boy the pole would be used to fly a pair of breeks (trousers), and if it was a girl, a small dress would be flown.

In the mid 1950s, the keepers and their families were moved to Edinburgh and the Signal Tower building was used as local authority housing for a time before it was converted into a museum during the early 1970s, opening on 1st August 1974.

No doubt many life and death dramas took place there, particularly during its period of service as a shore station for the lighthouse.

Checking Out the New Curator

In the mid 1980s, the then Curator, Mrs Margaret King, had just taken up her post at the Signal Tower. She was working late, waiting for the arrival of a group who had arranged to be shown round the Museum that evening.

Mrs King was sitting in the downstairs office and everything upstairs had been locked up. She became aware of the sound of someone typing, although the only typewriter was on one of the desks upstairs.

In her own words:

> This was before PCs and it was an old thumper of a machine. I wasn't worried but I thought I'd better go up and have a look. My previous dog, a lovely friendly gentle Labrador, usually welcomed everyone but she refused to come upstairs.
>
> Everything was as it should be upstairs and there was nothing amiss.
>
> I didn't feel ill at ease and it never happened again. It was as if something was just seeing who the new curator was and it was OK!
>
> I didn't think too much about it but happened to mention it to my predecessor who is a very down to earth, practical kind of person and she had had something similar happen to her.

Other members of the Signal Tower staff have also experienced strange goings on. One of the Museum Assistants has smelt what seemed like hot, buttered toast. When she mentioned this to her colleagues they admitted that on occasions they too had smelt what appeared to be the smell of baking.

On another occasion, the same Assistant was convinced that she heard a child's voice crying "Mummy", and she remains convinced that the cry was not her imagination at work.

Although she does not believe in spirits she is unable to give any explanation for her experiences.

It has been suggested that the smell of toast might have come from the restaurant across the road from the Museum but it would be stretching things in all respects to believe that such a smell could travel across the dual carriageway without being dispersed in the sea breezes.

There would appear be something about Angus Museums and the supernatural as the Meffan Museum in Forfar is also reputed to have a ghost, said to be a small boy who was sliding down the banister there when he fell to his death.

Mrs King was later based at the Meffan when she was Museums Manager but she admits that she never had any ghostly experiences there.

Apparently however, one of the cleaners refused to work in the building on her own because of the presence.

Brechin

There have also been reports of strange goings on at the Brechin Townhouse Museum.

The site was used for the Tolbooth from the middle of the 15th century until about 1790 when it was replaced by the present building.

In Scottish towns, the Tolbooth was literally that, the booth where tolls were collected. Through time, they became the centre of administration in the burghs, housing the council chambers, court-house and often a prison and the Tolbooth in Brechin would have been used for these purposes. The ground floor of the current building certainly was used as a shop, courtroom and debtors' prison and had two cells.

Whether any of those uses would have led to the building being haunted is not clear but it would seem that the Townhouse has a presence of some sort.

Lisa Carrie, who worked at the Museum as a Saturday assistant, had always debunked the idea of ghosts and the paranormal.

Her beliefs were challenged after an incident when she went to check the fire alarm. This required her to go through an alarmed door into part of the building which is off-limits to the public.

Lisa switched off the alarm and proceeded through the door. She must have carried out the operation correctly otherwise the alarm would have sounded when she opened the door.

Having carried out her check she made her way back to the main area. When she opened the door on her way out the alarm went off. On investigation, she found that the switch had been put back to the 'on' position and the only other member of staff present was at the front of the building.

Lisa is now less sure of her thoughts on the supernatural and admits that she always had a strange feeling of 'being watched' when working in the Townhouse.

Other members of staff have reported strange effects such as the kitchen being particularly cold during May or June even when the weather outside was quite warm. Sometimes, the staff have noticed vigorous movements of air on otherwise still days.

The cupboard adjacent to the kitchen smells damp and unpleasant while the figure of a child has been seen rising up from the floor of the cupboard and occasionally, the figure of an elderly man has also appeared.

One day, one of the security alarm sensors went off. There is nothing odd about that apart from the fact that only one sensor was activated. Not one of the intervening sensors which should have activated did so. If there is a security problem, all of the sensors should go off in sequence.

An engineer was called but he could find no fault and could not attribute the problem to dust particles.

Clerical Callers

The Library in Brechin is another site where members of the staff at all levels have had unexplained experiences. At least one former member of staff admitted to seeing an old woman wearing a navy or black shawl standing in what is now the computer section. She could only see the top part of the old woman who turned her head away. It was as if she was rather unhappy having been spotted or perhaps even about the fact that the library is there, on her territory.

Then, the figure slowly disappeared!

When the sighting was mentioned to another member of the staff she merely laughed and said, "That must be the ghost".

Such sightings are apparently quite common. Over the years, numerous members of the staff have reported seeing figures of monks making their way through the library. This is perhaps not too surprising as research suggests that in times past the area was walked regularly by the local clerics.

On other occasions the experience has been of sound rather than vision. During a meeting, held in what is now the children's area of the Library, footsteps could quite clearly be heard as if someone was walking through the building.

When someone went to investigate the noises stopped but they began again shortly afterwards.

There was no simple explanation and no possibility of the footsteps being made by staff members.

Footprints in the Snow

For one lady in Brechin a snowfall brought more than just a picturesque view.

There, in the snow lying on the path leading to her door were a set of footprints obviously, from the size of them, made by a child.

Disconcertingly for the woman they stopped before they reached her front door and there was no sign of footprints in the opposite direction.

A bizarre practical joke or a sign of paranormal activity, who can say? The same lady was on a troop train travelling through the Scottish Borders during World War II.

Her duties included serving hot tea to the servicemen and at one point she lifted up the kettle from the stove without realising that the handle would be hot. The pain from the burn was so great that she dropped the kettle and shouted out loudly, "Help, Mother".

Her own mother, who was walking along the beach at Montrose at the time, heard the shout. She even checked her watch and once the two were re-united it was confirmed as the exact moment when her daughter had dropped the hot kettle and shouted out a couple of hundred miles away.

There was snow on the ground when yet another strange incident happened in Brechin around 40 years ago.

An elderly man was looking out of his window at around 2.00am when he saw a man, dressed in old fashioned clothes, walk across the street and into the Trustee Savings Bank.

The onlooker reported his sighting to the police who investigated but they could find no trace of the mysterious intruder and, even more bizarrely, he had left no footprints in the snow!

The man who reported the incident was certain of what he saw as the figure was less than 100 yards away.

The City of Brechin is also home to unexplained lights that are seen flickering in the area down by the River Esk, particularly close to the Cathedral. Sometimes the lights appear strong while at other times they are feeble and weak and they seem to appear more during the summer months.

No logical explanation has ever been found for these sightings.

Montrose

During the early 1980s a young family living in one of the houses in Dorward Road experienced a series of strange events. While renovating the house it was found that metal bars had been used to secure the window of one of the upstairs bedrooms. These bars were removed when the room was modernised and re-decorated for the family's infant twin sons.

Two beds were placed in the room, one against the wall behind the entrance door. Shortly afterwards, when the twins were tucked up in to bed for the night, the infant placed in the bed against the wall began to scream and became hysterical. No amount of reassurance, coaxing or comforting would encourage him to go back to his bed. He kept pointing to the wall, indicating that something or someone was in the bed beside him.

The twins were still very young and had not developed comprehensive speech skills which made meaningful communication extremely difficult. As far as the parents were concerned it appeared that the infant had had a nightmare and, to alleviate his fears, they swapped the position of the beds the following evening, placing the other infant twin in the bed beside the wall.

The following evening the same situation was repeated only, this time, it was other infant twin, now placed in the bed against the wall, who had become hysterical and indicated that someone or something was in bed beside him.

Obviously, the parents were unsure what was really happening and discussed the children's strange behaviour with their family doctor. A few days later, in an effort to settle the children, the infants' beds were rearranged in the room away from the wall. This action appeared to solve the problem and the children slept soundly from that day onwards.

But that was not the end of the strange happenings. The family belonged to a local baby-sitting group that consisted of a number of young parents in the area, each taking turns to baby-sit for each other, thus allowing the parents some free time to go out for an evening.

Needless to say, the family never mentioned the occurrences to members of the group as any suggestion that there were mysterious goings-on in the house would have meant no baby-sitters.

Yet almost every time a baby-sitter sat for the family they informed the parents on their return that they had heard the sound of running footsteps on the upper floor. On each occasion the baby-sitter claimed, "It sounded as though a child was running from the bedroom across the upper landing to the toilet". On checking the children, they had always found them to be sound asleep.

Without revealing anything of the background, the couple discussed this phenomenon with the individual baby-sitters and found that at least nine different people had all had exactly the same experience.

The gas board, electric services, water board were all contacted to determine the source of the sounds but no natural or technical cause could be identified and these same disturbing events occurred every evening for many months and eventually escalated.

Footsteps on the Stairs

One evening, after checking that all the children were asleep, the mother settled downstairs to watch a film on television. She was certain that she heard footsteps as if someone had descended the stairs and then stopped outside the living room door. As no one was entering; she shouted, "Whoever you are, please come in". No one entered.

Assuming it was one of the children, she opened the door. Finding no one there, she ran upstairs to check on the children, only to find that they were all in bed and sound asleep.

Previously, the family had been aware that the wooden steps on their staircase were creaky. On this occasion, footsteps were heard descending the stairs but none ascending them again.

The mother knew that it could not have been one of her children who had come down the stairs and that she was alone downstairs. Realising that something strange and unnatural was occurring she suddenly became anxious and extremely tense.

Following these events, the history of the house and its occupants was researched. Information was provided by word of mouth from a reputable source (i.e. someone who knew the previous occupants and their family history).

Relating the story recently, the mother pointed out, "I cannot guarantee the total authenticity of the story as it may have become inadvertently embellished or forgotten throughout the years".

The story tells that the wife of a previous owner, a particularly well-to-do family, had given birth to twin boys. One child was both mentally and physically disabled and bars had been put over his bedroom window for his own safety.

In those days, there was a lot of stigma attached to anyone with birth defects or imperfections of any kind and society did not welcome them so this particular child was locked up in his bedroom and only allowed to run across the hall to the toilet. (The same route that the running footsteps were always heard.)

The other twin flourished in society and it was assumed that his disabled brother had died, presumably at birth but in fact the imprisoned child died as a young teenager.

It has always been assumed by the later family and their friends that removing the bars from the bedroom windows released the child's spirit and freed him from his imprisonment, although there might be a link through the fact that both families had twin boys.

Anyway, the most likely theory is that the spirit did not like other children using his 'space' in the bedroom and, as so often appears to happen in such cases, the infant children were able to see him, although he was apparently invisible to others.

The family discussed these events and confirmed other previous incidences with numerous bodies including the Church of Scotland. In view of the history of the house and the recurring events, the Church of Scotland determined that exorcism was required. A county Bishop from another denomination who had experience of such matters was contacted and he, along with a local Church of Scotland minister, called one evening to perform an exorcism of the house and particularly the children's bedroom.

According to the children's mother, "These events occurred more than 23 years ago and I believe there have been no further occurrences since".

Regular Visitors

The Bridge Street area of Montrose seems to have a number of spirits who regularly visit the properties there.

Members of one family who live in the area are certain that the spirit of a little girl lives with them. They believe she was regularly locked in a closet when she was naughty but she is apparently happy in the house and has no wish to leave.

In their previous home they also had regular visits from a nun who was often seen standing over the cradle while their daughter slept.

The young lady in question, now a grown woman, has seen the spirit that seems to watch over her but still doesn't believe.

Another Montrose couple spent the first months of their married life in an attic flat in Bridge Street. One night, the husband was awakened by the feeling that he was being pulled towards the bay window by an invisible source. The force was so great that he had to grab hold of the bed head to prevent himself being pulled out through the window.

This happened several years ago but, asked about the incident even now, the husband is still convinced that it actually happened and that, whatever it was, the experience certainly wasn't just a nightmare or bad dream.

When the incident occurred, he decided not to tell his wife about the experience as he didn't want to upset her.

At the time, he was a student working nights in Chivers, the local canning factory.

One morning he came home and his wife asked if he had come home during the night as she had wakened to find a dark figure, just as he might have looked in his overalls, standing over her.

If that was not disconcerting enough, she then heard what seemed to be her own voice coming from the figure asking gruffly, "Who are you?" Such an apparition isn't uncommon with certain spirits, apparently unable to accept that they no longer have a place on Earth, believing that someone else is living in their property.

Ghostly Guests

Another of the big houses in Montrose appears to have a number of non-paying guests.

An old dinner gong, long since discarded and relegated to the attic, is sometimes heard to sound. Despite investigations, no explanation can be found as to how the gong is struck.

Members of staff often see figures walking up corridors in front of them only to turn the corner and then apparently disappear. When such sightings are mentioned to colleagues they often respond that they were not on that particular floor at that time so making the appearances all the more difficult to explain.

Residents have also had strange experiences saying they see and hear children playing even when there are no children in the house.

A number of years ago, Montrose dancing teacher Robina Addison was in her home in Melville Gardens in the town when she first spotted a young girl, dressed in Victorian garb, standing behind her.

She could see her quite clearly, including the flowers, forget-me-nots, in her hair. Almost as if she realised she had been spotted, the figure walked away and disappeared through the wall into another room.

The girl was seen on one further occasion but since then she has never re-appeared.

A previous owner of the house, internationally renowned artist, Dr James Morrison, also recalls smelling pipe smoke in the property on a number of occasions. No one in the house smoked and he also knew that his neighbour was not a smoker either.

Was a previous resident making himself known to the present occupiers?

Factory Phantoms

In an office on the industrial estate off Coronation Avenue in Montrose a manager was shocked to see a figure dressed in what appeared to be military uniform sitting in the chair beside his desk.

It was not the first time he had seen the figure. Earlier, when about to lock up after working late, he had seen the silhouette of the figure, which he described as wearing a heavy greatcoat, either fitted or belted at the waist. The trousers too were made of heavy material that 'sat well' rather than flopping.

He described the facial features as indistinct rather than blank. Somewhat alarmed, the manager then looked away and when he looked back the figure had disappeared.

This was just one of a number of odd occurrences in the building. While working late one night the manager suddenly found all the telephones ringing at once and he was unable to get an outside line. A technical fault perhaps? The matter was investigated by telephone engineers who could find nothing wrong with the system.

On a number of occasions lights were found burning in parts of the building where he knew, for certain, that they had been switched off.

One instance of that was when he had been summoned to the building because of a problem with the alarm system. He was waiting for the engineer to arrive and had gone outside to get something from his car. When he went back into the building he found the lights on again and, after he had switched them off, he found that they had come on yet again.

The problems do not merely relate to the lights. Doors, which have been securely locked, are found to be open. Documents left on the manager's desk are sometimes found scattered around while other items in the room move about during periods when the office is securely locked. Simple explanations such as draughts have been discounted.

On one occasion, a pot plant was discovered sitting in the middle of the floor.

He was equally concerned too to find that a memo, relating to the observation of the minute's silence at 11am on Remembrance Day, which he knew had been near the bottom of a pile of correspondence, had moved and was in full view at the top.

Other items, such as keys and jackets, are regularly moved from where he knows for certain they have been left. Having locked himself in the building one evening the manager was shocked and surprised when the keys that he had just left in the lock were 'thrown' past him as he walked away.

Perhaps equally frightening was hearing his Christian name called out when he knew he was alone on the premises.

Other members of the staff have experienced strange happenings and seen the figure too. One employee had a door wrenched from his grasp and tradesmen working in the building often remark on people being present when the staff themselves know that no one else is in the area.

Sometimes staff can smell sweet pipe tobacco in the building and the manager confesses that he sometimes unwittingly finds himself following the smell.

Noises are heard from inside even when there is no one left in the building. Footsteps are regularly heard and doors have been known to open and bang shut when locked!

Pushy Presences

Perhaps the most frightening experience for the manager was when he was physically pushed against his desk with such force that he was left bruised and shaken.

The manager himself has a number of theories. He feels that the happenings may stem from alterations that have been carried out to the building although the premises, like the others on the estate, are relatively new, so any paranormal activity cannot be readily traced to the re-awakening of incidents that previously took place there. In fact, until the 60s or 70s the area was completely undeveloped.

There would also appear to be increased activity starting around early November which makes him wonder if there is some military connection relating to Remembrance Day as the industrial estate is close to the site of the former airfield at Montrose.

Another employee has reported similar experiences. He looked into a rest room only to see a figure lounging in a chair. The apparition faded very quickly before the employee could see his face but he did notice that it was wearing a short jacket with an astrakhan collar – a flying jacket perhaps?

At the other end of the building, beside one of the doors, an employee was pushed with sufficient force to send him across the room. Other people present thought he had stumbled but he is adamant that he was pushed.

Just outside another door in the building, the same employee stepped back and bumped into someone standing behind him. He turned to apologise, only to discover that there was no one there!

On at least two other occasions, an invisible person has brushed past the same employee and the cleaner has also reported being nudged or bumped on a number of occasions.

There have also been instances of heavy double doors moving, as if someone had recently gone through them. The employee who reported this knew that he was the only person in the building.

He could also discount the effect of a draught. No windows or doors were open and, in any case, the weight of the doors is such that moving them requires a considerable amount of force.

Like the manager, he too has noted that these events seem to be more frequent around Remembrance Sunday and he too feels that a connection with the former RAF Montrose seems likely.

That said, investigations into the previous use of the ground suggest that it was nothing more than a field during World War II.

Charleton House

Just about a mile north of Montrose, on the A92 to Aberdeen, lie the lands of Charleton. Around the beginning of the 12th century, the estate, together with the salmon fishing on the North Esk, was granted to Sir David de Graham by King William the Lion.

It is likely that the estate would have included some sort of fortification and later, once the need for such things had passed, a manor house.

The Graham family, which later included the Marquis of Montrose, held the land, along with a number of neighbouring estates, until the 1600s when Charleton was sold to James Scott of Logie.

It then passed through a number of hands before being bought by the Carnegies of Pitarrow in December 1767. Susan Carnegie, née Scott, the lady who was responsible for the establishment of the lunatic asylum in Montrose, was the wife of George Carnegie.

After the estate passed from the Carnegie family it had a series of owners, including the More-Gordons and the Wilkies.

During World War II the House was used as a billet for Polish soldiers who vacated the premises in 1946 and it was put to yet another use with the setting up of the National Health Service in Britain two years later.

The plan was the brainchild of Sir William Beveridge whose report was published in 1942. Obviously, little could be done until the War was over but, with the 1945 election producing a Labour Government under Clement Attlee, suddenly the possible became achievable. Attlee appointed Aneurin Bevan as Minister for Health and he was given the task of introducing this major reform.

There was quite a bit of resistance from within the health services but, eventually, the objections were overcome and the NHS began on 5th July 1948.

To provide maternity services in Montrose, Charleton House was purchased in 1946 and fitted out for its new purpose.

It was opened on Friday 2nd July 1948, although Charleton was in fact some weeks away from accepting patients, and continued as the maternity hospital for north-east Angus until it finally closed in the late 70s.

After it was vacated by the Health Service there were a number of plans to develop the house and grounds and it looked for a time as if it would become an hotel.

In fact, it was used as a refugee centre for Vietnamese boat people before it became vacant again and after at least two major fires it was declared unsafe and was eventually demolished.

Extra Staff

Given the long history of the estate it is not surprising that the House was reputed to be haunted, although what might be surprising is the fact that the spirits all appear to be from recent times.

My informant, one of the midwives who worked at Charleton Maternity Home, told me that there were a number of apparent sightings of spirits during that time.

On one occasion, after finishing her normal shift, she had been asked if she would stay on to provide extra cover. She was lying sleeping in one of the staff bedrooms when she heard a noise like a rolled up ball of wool hitting her door. There was no apparent explanation for the noise and she told me that she stayed in bed and did not seek to investigate!

One day, as she walked down one of the corridors, she passed a figure looking into one of the many cupboards. She thought she knew who it was and as it was someone she wanted to have a word with she turned back only to find that the figure had disappeared.

Such sightings appear to have been common. When passing by the day room she noticed a woman in a dressing gown watching television but all the patients were accounted for and she couldn't work out who the mystery woman might be. When she went back to look for her the figure had vanished.

Another unexplained incident happened during the Christmas holidays. Because of the time of year as many patients as possible had been sent home. The few who were still in the Home were all asleep and there were only two staff members on duty.

One member of staff thought she could hear the sound of her colleague's footsteps upstairs. Strangely enough, at the same time the other member of staff could hear footsteps on the floor below.

Each thought that they were hearing the other's footsteps. It was only when one of them remarked on it that they each discovered that they had both removed their shoes so as not to make any noise and disturb anyone. Whatever the source of the footsteps was, it was not either of them.

Interestingly enough, many of the figures were dressed in what appeared to be nurses' uniforms, making it seem as if the spirits were themselves nurses, although there are no clues as to who they might be or why they were there.

There was one other strange incident when one of the mothers insisted on being discharged as she had had a premonition that the Home was to burn down. It did of course, but at a much later date.

Another Disappearing Figure

Several years ago, a Montrose keep-fit enthusiast was running along the beach near the town. He had reached the River North Esk and was now running back towards the town

As he ran, he noticed a man in an old-fashioned boiler suit walking towards him. The man had on sturdy shoes, again possibly old fashioned, rather than boots, and his hair was cut in an old style. The man looked real enough and certainly didn't appear in any way to be ghost like.

The runner nodded or spoke to the figure, he can't remember which now, but got no response and yet he had no sense of being ignored.

After passing the figure, the runner, taking the route he usually did, climbed up the dunes and, when he reached the top, he looked back but the figure had disappeared. This surprised him, as there were few, if any, places where the man could have gone.

Sometime later, the runner was making his way along the same stretch of beach at around the same time of day when he came face to face with the man again.

Again the runner acknowledged the presence of the man and received no reply and, as he climbed the dunes, he saw that the figure had again disappeared.

Thinking back on the incidents and how the figure was dressed now he wonders if the man might have had some association with the old airfield at Montrose.

Certainly, he still cannot properly explain the man's sudden disappearance, leaving him only with the explanation that he might just have come face to face with one of the airfield's many ghosts.

The Turk's Head

Back in February 1997 a lady driver was waiting in traffic on George Street in Montrose.

As she sat patiently in her car she saw an elderly man making his way up the street. What first drew her attention to the man was the way he was dressed as he appeared to be from a different age with his homespun jacket and old fashioned cap or bonnet.

She was stationary for some time and was able to form a picture of the figure who was of slim build and slightly stooped. He walked slowly and then turned towards what was then a boarded up shop. Just as the lady thought there was no point in him looking in the shop because it was closed the figure disappeared through the boarded up window.

Although the driver had never had an experience of that kind before she was in no doubt as to what she had witnessed.

Interviewed at the time of the sighting, a lady who lived above the shop said she had not had any experiences of ghostly figures but did smell sweet tobacco and ladies perfume on occasions, always in the same part of her house.

The shop itself was situated on what was originally the site of the Turk's Head Inn and stables, which were demolished in the early 19th century to allow the roadway, the 'Shuilbred' (or narrow vennel), to be widened to form George Street.

So perhaps this particular spirit was looking for a spirit of another kind or some other refreshment in his favourite howff.

Arbroath Apparitions

A number of years ago, Mary McVey lived in Hill Street in Arbroath. As she lay in bed she often felt that someone had got into bed beside her. Although, at that time, her husband Bob regularly worked away from home on oil rigs, she has always been certain that it was him who got into bed and put his arm around her, just as he does when he is at home.

On another occasion she awoke to be confronted by a tall dark shadowy figure that moved towards the bed before stopping at the door. It looked over towards her and then simply disappeared. Recalling the story now she thinks the figure may have been that of a monk but she remembers being absolutely terrified. Certainly, monk-like figures seem to be regular visitors to houses around the Abbey, which would not be at all surprising.

Perhaps another spirit who felt that there were strangers living in his property?

These are not Mary's only experiences of spirit visitors. Back staying in her parent's home at one point she was sharing a room with her recently widowed sister and her son when she awoke to see her sister's late husband staring down at his wife and son. He turned towards Mary and put his finger to his lips, as if asking her to remain silent, before disappearing.

That was the only occasion on which he appeared to Mary but his wife saw him regularly.

Mary also stayed for a time in India Lane in Montrose where she saw a figure passing by one of the glass doors in the house one day. Bob was outside working in their garden at the time and Mary assumed he had come back into the house to get something. It was only later when she asked him why he had come inside and he told her he had been outside all the time and hadn't returned to the house until then that she realised she had seen evidence of another spirit.

Sometime later she discovered that a previous owner of the property had died after her chip pan caught fire.

Lunan Lodge

OS Map, sheet 54: NO 687526

Lunan Lodge is situated between Montrose and Arbroath, just off the A92 road that connects the two burghs.

A former Manse for the ministers of Lunan Church, the Lodge was built in 1749 and extended in 1800, 1860 and 1970, before becoming the home of the May family, Samantha and Jules, who run it as a bed and breakfast business.

The house offers fine views over the coast and Samantha and Jules fell in love with it immediately.

Jules has a science background and was unwilling at first to accept that there was anything odd about the house but it soon became apparent that guests experienced strange happenings. What was most intriguing about the stories was that, despite the fact that none of the guests knew each other or the history of the house, the tales they told were remarkably consistent with each one giving similar descriptions of what they had seen.

The spirit is a man the Mays believe is called George Smith. He appears very clearly, so much so that on occasions they have spoken to him, and he was standing in the kitchen when the couple first arrived in the house.

George believed, and still believes, that the house is his and as a result he tells people to get out.

During the early part of the 20th century, Samantha and Jules told me, the minister was a man called William Macdonald. He went off to the First World War and failed to return but his widow was permitted to stay on in the Manse and, presumably to make ends meet, she took in a number of lodgers including George.

Before long, George considered himself to be the man of the house and believed that the Manse, and possibly even Mrs Macdonald, was his property.

When she died, he claimed that the house was his and he was eventually convicted of fraud for his pains.

Nevertheless, it seems he is still of that opinion to this day and he appears regularly to guests and invites them to leave his property.

Another spirit that frequents the Lodge is Madeleine, a former maid. She appears, as one might expect, only in the old part of the house where she can be seen, walking through walls, presumably where there were doors during her lifetime, and avoiding obstructions that would have been there in her day.

In 1906, a rider at the property was thrown from his horse and killed. His niece, a spirit called Amy or Emily, has been contacted and will answer questions about the accident, although she speaks in a strange dialect.

Babies put down in one of the rooms often cry and are unwilling to sleep, as if they are afraid of something or someone there beside them. The solution is to instruct the spirit, quietly but firmly, to leave. This, Samantha says, works a treat and the baby will drop off to sleep within minutes.

Several other strange phenomena have been observed. Footsteps are regularly heard walking on the gravel and guests have been known to look for the 'owner' of the footsteps, only to find to their surprise that, although they come closer, no one ever appears.

Monks and druids have been seen at the foot of the garden and one of the former ministers and his wife have been seen clearly enough to be sketched. The couple were later caught on video.

Not only humans seem to be able to see the spirits. Samantha and Jules' two cats are sometimes seen staring at or following the progress of an invisible presence around the room. Although one might stare vacantly into space the couple suggest it is unlikely that both cats would do this towards the same spot at the same time as they sometimes do.

Hide and Seek with Spirits

In a house such as the Lodge there is ample space for children to play hide and seek and games have often raised the possibility of there being more participants than the youngsters appreciate.

Often such games are interrupted by claims that people have been spotted only to find that the 'target' was in fact in another room. The spirit usually involved is a stable boy known as Jacob and his dog Ben. For whatever reason, Jacob is frightened of the occupants of the house and he hides from them. The figure of Jacob has been seen taking refuge behind the desk in the office during a game of hide and seek. When the searcher challenged the disappearing figure as it hid behind the office desk, believing it to be her quarry, she was surprised to find that there was no one there.

Several investigations have been carried out at Lunan Lodge by various ghost investigation groups and none have left disappointed. Psychics have reported different experiences and EMF (electro magnetic field) meters often give strange readings which may indicate the presence of something otherwise unseen.

On a number of occasions investigators have found that battery operated equipment wouldn't work because recently charged batteries had been inexplicably drained of power. One television company only just managed to complete filming before their last battery, which should have lasted for 24 hours, gave out, like the previous batteries, after just minutes of filming.

Strangely enough, guests have reported the opposite effect too, with mobile telephones that normally require constant recharging retaining their charge for much longer during their stay at the Lodge.

Despite its idyllic setting, Lunan Lodge has an air of mystery surrounding it and, although Samantha and Jules are a couple who take a very logical approach to life, they too are at a loss to explain some of the happenings there.

Lunan Lodge provides accommodation on a bed & breakfast basis, including giving guests the chance to sleep in the 'Shouty Man' room and be awarded a certificate for their bravery. Further details from the website <www.lunanlodge.co.uk/haunted-house.htm> or telephone 01241 830679.

Ethie Castle

OS Map, sheet 54: NO 688468

Just across Lunan Bay from Lunan Lodge is Ethie Castle, which is believed to be the second oldest building in Scotland with a history of unbroken occupation, there having been a building on the site from about 1100 (**18**). The present sandstone building dates from the 14th century when the site formed part of the estates of Arbroath Abbey. Later, Ethie passed into the hands of the de Maxwell family before reverting to the Abbey.

In 1524 Cardinal David Beaton became the Commendator of Arbroath and Ethie was one of a number of properties that he owned and occupied at different times.

Beaton lived at Ethie with Marion Ogilvie from Melgund Castle, another of his properties. According to the religious beliefs of the time Beaton should, of course, have been celibate but he and Marion were reputed to have had several children together.

The Cardinal was well known in Scotland for his efforts to suppress the 'heretics' who proposed to reform the Roman Catholic Church and it was his vicious policy towards them which eventually brought about his own death.

One of the Reformers was George Wishart from Pitarrow in nearby Kincardineshire who, as well as being a preacher of the reformed faith, taught at the Grammar School in Montrose.

Cardinal Beaton had Wishart arrested, tried and condemned to death and he was put to death at St Andrews in 1546.

Wishart was only one of a number of reformers who had been executed on the orders of Beaton and a band of Protestant sympathisers took revenge by murdering the Cardinal in St Andrews in May of that year.

18 *Ethie Castle; Cardinal Beaton can be heard dragging his gout affected leg.*

Beaton was reputed to suffer from gout and his ghost is said to haunt Ethie Castle, his footsteps making a strange sound due to him walking normally on one foot but dragging his gout afflicted leg.

On one occasion, a youngster who was staying in the Castle in the 1960s or 70s went exploring with his brother. He heard unexplained noises and saw a flickering light. Although he initially suspected that it was just his brother trying to scare him he eventually realised that it could not be his brother who was responsible for the sight and sounds so he made haste back to a more congenial area of the Castle only to be told that he had probably come across the ghost of the Cardinal.

In fact, thanks to the late I A N Henderson, author of *Discovering Angus & Mearns*, we have a description of the Cardinal, or at least of his ghost, 'a very small, fat, red-faced man in a red gown with a cord tied around his ample middle and with a foot wrapped up in flannel'.

The description certainly sounds just how we would imagine Beaton might look. Perhaps the word imagine is too close to the truth on this occasion but it may be a genuine eye-witness account although the source is not clear.

In 1665 the castle was purchased by the Carnegies who were later to become the Earls of Northesk. The 7th Earl, William Carnegie, was third in command under Nelson at the Battle of Trafalgar and his part in the Battle resulted in him being awarded honours by the King and both Houses of Parliament.

Later, the novelist Sir Walter Scott stayed at Ethie as a guest of the 8th Earl and the Castle is believed to be the inspiration for the Castle of Knockwinnock in *The Antiquary*.

The property remained in the Carnegies' hands until 1928 when it was bought by a gentleman called Cunningham-Hector, splendidly described as, 'a man of independent means, not trade'.

It was his family's nanny who reputedly heard a child crying and the sounds of a child walking along, as if pushing an old-fashioned baby walker or toy.

Sometime around 1930, the remains of a child, along with a wooden cart, were found, bricked up in a wall of the Castle but after the remains were given a proper burial the noises were never heard again.

Time for the Supernatural

One of the big mysteries in the Castle concerns the Regency clock which belongs to the current owners. It sits in the dining room, its pendulum is broken, the key has long since been lost and, consequently, it simply doesn't work.

What is strange however is that sometimes the hands move to the hour all by themselves and the chimes are heard, as if a child was playing with the timepiece just to hear it chiming.

This has been observed by several guests staying at Ethie.

Another guest left her book behind when she went upstairs to see if her husband was ready to come down for dinner. Later, she thanked the staff for taking her book into the dining room for her. Only none of them had moved the book!

In the Castle itself, two members of staff have each heard a voice saying "Hello". Each assumed it was the other speaking but in fact neither had.

There are tales too of a green lady being seen in the walled garden at Ethie. When she is seen sobbing, it is a sign that someone connected with the Castle is about to die.

Perhaps the strangest manifestation at Ethie is the reported sight of a file of monks climbing up a now non-existent staircase on one of the outside walls of the building.

During my visit, the current owner, Mrs de Morgan, also showed me a particularly strange artefact that she found in the Castle. It is an old piece of rope with a label attached.

According to the label, the rope was used by smugglers to suspend an exciseman over a low ledge near Red Head. The man had been blindfolded but could hear the waves roaring below.

The exciseman held until he was totally exhausted and unable to hold on any longer. He released his grip on the rope and fell to the ground, a distance of only two feet.

Nevertheless, when he was picked up he was found to be dead. It would not be surprising if his spirit roams the cliffs in the area looking for the smugglers whose bizarre 'joke' caused his death.

> Ethie Castle is now a private house although it does accommodate paying guests. Further details can be obtained from the website <www.ethiecastle.com> or by telephoning 01241 830434.

Claypotts Castle OS Map, sheet 54: NO 451319

Claypotts Castle near Dundee is also supposed to have a connection with Cardinal Beaton. An apparition known as the 'White Lady', thought to be Beaton's lover, Marion Ogilvie, is reputed to wave a white handkerchief from one of the upper windows on the 29th May each year, the anniversary of Beaton's death.

This is an unlikely tale as the building of Claypotts Castle was not started until 1569, over 20 years after Beaton's murder, and, in any case, Marion Ogilvie lived at Melgund.

Claypotts is also supposed to have been the home of a brownie, a benevolent spirit which is reputed to perform light household duties in its chosen abode in return for small gifts.

As ever, the brownie enthusiastically carried out its household chores but this one had very high standards.

Unfortunately, the other members of the staff at the castle were not so efficient and eventually the brownie got fed up with their sloppy ways.

The last straw came apparently in February 1849 when one of the female servants was asked to collect some greens from the kitchen garden to make 'kail brose', a cabbage broth. The girl given the task was careless and, instead of selecting the best leaves, she just picked the first that came to hand.

This exasperated the poor brownie so much that she followed the servant into one of the darker corridors where she snatched the greens from the hapless girl and proceeded to set about her, striking her with the miserable leaves.

Having administered its punishment to the servant lass the brownie took its leave of Claypotts Castle and was never seen again but, as it left, the brownie recited a rhyme:

> The Ferry and the Ferry-well;
> The Camp and the Camp-hill;
> Balmossie and Balmossie-mill;
> Burnside and Burns-hill;
> The thin sowens o' Drumgeith;
> The fair May o' Monifieth;
> There's Gutherston and Wallaceton!
> Claypotts I'll gie my malison; [curse]
> Come I late or come I ear,
> Ballunie's boards are aye bare.

The brownie's curse was presumably that those involved would never prosper.

There is also a legend suggests that there is an underground tunnel, approximately a mile long, which links Broughty Castle to Claypotts. A piper is reputed to have strayed into the tunnel and, having failed to find his way out, can still sometimes be heard playing in the bowels of the earth, a tale which is certainly far from unusual as we shall hear.

Melgund Castle

At some point during the middle of the 15th century, a guard was keeping watch from the ramparts of Melgund Castle. It was a dismal night, 'dreich' as Scots would say, and the unfortunate man had difficulty in keeping his spirits up.

As he looked out over the surrounding area for any signs of his master's enemies all he could see was a frozen and deserted landscape covered in snow with no noise other than the howling of a starving wolf.

His courage was not in doubt. He had been a soldier but, somehow, nothing he did could lift his mood that night.

As the hours dragged past there was nothing for him to see until suddenly, out of the darkness, he saw a hearse drawn by four black horses. As it made its way towards the Castle he could see that it was being followed by a host of lords and knights on horseback and, behind them, a procession of vassals and serfs on foot.

Such was his fear that he could scarcely move over to the side of the ramparts above the main gate where the hearse had stopped.

As the hearse moved off, the Castle bell started to toll, signalling the death of one of the residents.

Some time earlier, the Laird, Sir David Lindsay, knowing that he was dying, had asked for the local priest to attend him.

Lindsay had always mocked and scorned the Church but with his end near, he hoped to make his peace with his Maker.

He asked for his close family, who had been at his bedside, to leave so that he could speak to the priest alone and then he confessed to his wickedness.

He had never married his first wife although she had believed that they were married. What was even worse was that he had poisoned her and their child. They had been buried in the same grave and he had gone to their funeral making much pretence of being the grieving husband.

Every night since, a vision of his late wife and child appeared to him although his present wife had no knowledge of his past or of the apparitions.

Lindsay admitted that he had much more on his conscience but he died before he could complete his confession.

Before the priest left the Castle, the guard spoke to him about the vision he had seen. The churchman explained to him that he had been favoured by Heaven but also told him that this was a reminder that he should lead a holy and pure life.

The guard returned to his own home where he recounted his tale to his wife who in turn told him that she had had a vision too. As she slept she had dreamt that she had been visited by a lady dressed in white with an infant in her arms. Behind her, there had been a knight with a cup in his hands.

The lady turned and took the cup, drank from it and fell down, apparently dead. The infant also appeared to be dead. As they lay there, the knight smiled as if satisfied that his evil plan had achieved its objective.

Six days later the funeral of Sir David Lindsay took place, exactly as the guard had first 'seen' it from the ramparts.

In later years, Melgund was owned by Cardinal Beaton and his paramour Marion Ogilvie before passing to the Murray family who were merchants in Dundee.

One dark winter's night in 1716, the Murray family simply disappeared, leaving the castle fully lit and a full meal on the table ready for eating. A number of theories persisted about the family's sudden disappearance. Some said that the Laird had drink and gambling problems and that, having lost his fortune, he and his family had literally done a moonlight flit, while others reckoned they had taken what remained of their wealth and hidden in an underground vault at the Castle.

Yet another theory was that he became too heavily involved with the Jacobite cause and, hearing that a Royalist Army under the Duke of Argyll was heading towards his stronghold, decided to make himself and his family scarce.

Ignoring any supernatural involvement, Murray and his family probably travelled to Montrose and took a ship from there to a European country but no matter why or how the Murrays disappeared they were certainly never seen in the neighbourhood again.

Years later, a young man from Aberlemno was reputed to have found the entrance to the family's secret vault. The experience does not appear to have been a happy one as he said he had seen things he hoped he would never see on earth again and he gave no indication as to whether he had seen the family or the treasure they had reputedly taken with them.

Shortly afterwards, the entrance to the vault collapsed so the young man was unable to return, even if he had wanted to.

Kinnaird Castle   OS Map, sheet 54: NO 634571

Kinnaird Castle, which lies midway between Brechin and Montrose, is the scene of another interesting paranormal tale.

James Carnegie, the second Earl of Southesk, was apparently known as the Black Earl because of his swarthy complexion but the nickname may also have been a reference to his love of the black arts.

James attended the University of Padua, where, as an advanced student, he was reputed to have learnt the ways of darkness from no less an expert than the Devil, Auld Nick himself.

As one might imagine, this was no ordinary class and the fee for taking part was that the last student to leave the classroom on particular days selected by the Devil would have to 'pay' by giving him his soul.

Eventually, Carnegie was chosen but, being particularly quick witted, he pointed out that that his shadow had been last out the door. Satan, with his love of all things dark, accepted.

Forever afterwards, the Second Earl never cast a shadow and was said to have constantly moved about in the shade to avoid others noticing this peculiarity.

It was when James died on a wild and stormy night in 1669 that the Devil was supposed to have finally claimed his prize. The Black Earl's body is said to have been taken away in a coach pulled by six coal black horses, which carried the Earl to the Starney-Bucket Well which lay in the appropriately named De'il's Den to the south of the family burial vault.

According to local legend, on wild, stormy nights the coach repeats its dreadful journey, driving at a gallop from the house towards the old burial ground where it disappears.

Vayne Castle

OS Map, sheet 54: NO 494599

The Castle of Vayne was an impressive three storey structure with a grand circular tower in the south west corner, built on the north bank of the River Noran It eventually came into the ownership of the Southesk family and the Black Earl's son Robert is credited with restoring it to a very high standard.

At one time, Vayne, or the old manor house of Fern as it was also known, was said to have belonged to our old friend Cardinal Beaton and was believed to be where he retired, 'for less consistent purposes than the fulfilment of his vow of celibacy'.

On the River Noran close to the Castle there is a deep pool known as Tommy's Pot.

The name is said to have come from the fact that a son of the Cardinal and Lady Vayne is reputed to have drowned there. While this is an interesting tale there is no evidence that Beaton owned any property in the district or that he ever dallied with Lady Vayne.

Once Vayne was deserted it fell into disrepair and, as so often happens with old buildings, the stone was put to other uses by the neighbouring population.

Another legend is that, before the family left the building, they hid all their valuables in a deep dungeon under the castle.

The possibility of finding treasure brought hordes of fortune hunters to the ruins and one such individual is believed to have found the entrance to the dungeon. He was on the point of claiming his prize when a monster in the shape of a horned ox thrust him out of the way before disappearing through a hole in the wall. The entrance to the dungeon then closed before the treasure seeker's eyes and was lost forever.

The area around Vayne is a popular haunt for the Devil according to a local rhyme:

> There's the Brownie o' Ba'quharn,
> An the Ghaist o' Brandieden;
> But of a' the places i' the parish,
> The deil burns up the Vayne!

East of Vayne Castle there is a large chunk of sandstone marked with what appears to be a giant footprint. Although known locally as the kelpie's footmark, the mark is reckoned to have been made by the Devil when he used the stepping-stones.

One of his favourite pastimes was to cry for help in the terrified manner of a drowning victim to lure unsuspecting passers-by into the river.

But the best known spirits found in the area are the brownie and the ghaist (ghost) mentioned in the rhyme. Indeed, many of the locals believed them to be one and the same.

At nearby Brandyden, there lived a tyrannical landlord who regularly terrorised his tenants. One unfortunate so incurred his wrath that he was thrown into a dungeon to await execution. The tenant died a natural death before the cruel sentence could be carried out and he was buried close to the castle.

From that day on, the landlord was plagued by ill-luck and strange happenings. Doors and windows mysteriously opened by themselves and unexplained screaming was often heard throughout the building. As a result, the landlord was unable to keep his servants and he himself eventually died a sudden and mysterious death.

The tenant's spirit, freed of its mission for revenge, changed character and, in the manner of a brownie, began assisting the local farmer's wife with her chores.

The idea that the brownie and the friendly ghost are one and the same is found in a poem entitled 'The Ghaist of Ferne-den'.

It describes how the farmer's wife took ill in childbirth. No one was inclined to go for help in case they met the ghost so the brownie himself saddled 'the auld mare' and went to get the Mammy (midwife).

He rode with her back to the farmhouse, although she was afraid of meeting the ghost. The poem ends with his perhaps, less than re-assuring, words to the midwife:

> "But gin they Victo [ask], wha brocht you here?
> Cause they were scarce o' men;
> Just tell them that ye rade ahint
> The Ghaist o' Ferne-den!"

More Arbroath Apparitions

Muriel Mc...... of Arbroath lived for a time in a maisonette in St Vigeans Road, Arbroath, part of a block in which six houses had been converted into four.

She first noticed strange happenings in the house when she became aware of a wraith-like shadow following her about the house and, although she described it as being indistinct, she believed it to be that of a man or boy.

Her husband died very suddenly just after this incident and she still wonders if this apparition was in fact a portent of his death.

Later, her elder daughter awoke one night to find that she seemed to have a heavy weight pressing down on top of her.

This might have been put down to a nightmare but Muriel had occasion to sleep in the same room and she had exactly the same experience. Telling the story, she says she had to use all of her inner strength to get up because of the weight.

When I suggested that sceptics might claim that this is a normal experience which can happen when someone wakes up she pointed out that she has never had a similar experience anywhere else or at any other time.

Her younger daughter, who was then aged about six or seven, saw a young boy, whom she took to be about 14 or 15, apparently emerge from a cupboard and go into the middle bedroom where these experiences seemed to happen. She can still recall the incident and says that the boy had ginger hair.

The middle bedroom seems to have been a centre of the unexplained as she recounted how the light used to go on and off on its own. As children, they thought this was fun and they would put the light on and close the door, only to find on opening the door moments later that it had turned itself off.

Thinking about her experiences now, she believes that the spirit was a horrid evil one, a fact that she bases on the incidents involving people waking up feeling as if there were heavy weights on top of them in that room.

She conceded that there was no poltergeist activity but insisted that she had nightmares as a child which happened only when she slept in that particular room.

Muriel recalled finding a Bible that had been left in the property. The name inside was Daniel Munro, aged 14, although she cannot link it with any of the happenings in the house.

There have been instances too of other people experiencing smells in the house. Muriel says that on one occasion she could smell soup being heated although it wasn't from her house and she is certain that it was not coming from any of the neighbouring properties.

On another occasion she heard a cough and smelt pipe tobacco. Her late husband had been a pipe smoker.

Attempts by the family to investigate the history of the building have come to nothing. They think that a woman may have died in a fire in the building, although they cannot even be certain of that fact.

The family have moved a number of times since experiencing these strange happenings but there has never been any repeat of the mysterious events!

A Family Phantom?

Lesley Martin is a young mum living in Arbroath. She also appears to attract the paranormal, having had a number of experiences which defy explanation.

As a young girl living at home in Bernard Crescent, Arbroath with her Mum, she recalls seeing the figure of a small man leaning on her bedroom door. Dressed in a welder's cap, worn back to front, and an overall or boiler suit, he smiled at her and she says she was in no way frightened. The figure remained in sight for three or four seconds before fading away.

When she told her mother and grandmother about what she had seen her grandmother told her that that was exactly how her late husband dressed for his work at the Northern Tool & Gear, an engineering works in the town.

Not all of Lesley's experiences have been just as benign however. She talks of having brushes thrown at her in the bathroom and how one day, while she was on the stairs, a picture 'flew' past her.

Her Mum also found strange things happening in the house. A guitar, lying in the corner of a room with no one near it, suddenly strummed itself. She asked it to do it again and lo and behold it did.

The family had a bull mastiff dog and when Lesley's Mum thought she heard someone coming in to the house the dog rushed past her to the door. There was no one there, in fact the door was locked, but when her Mum got to the door but she found the dog cowering and whimpering in a corner. After the incident it refused to go back upstairs.

Another oddity in the house is the disappearing picture. Like most grandmothers, Lesley's Mum proudly keeps pictures of her grandchildren out on display. One particular picture constantly disappears from its normal place before re-appearing somewhere else. The family are satisfied that it is not one of them playing a cruel practical joke and no reasonable explanation can be found for the picture moving.

The house sometimes has an unexplained smell of rotten eggs.

When she was 18, Lesley moved to a flat of her own in Arbroath's Arbirlot Road West. If she believed that she had left the paranormal behind her she was soon to be put right when, within a few months of moving, she encountered a new set of strange experiences.

At one point, a cassette tape which had been sitting on a display unit flew past her head. She can give no explanation for that at all.

Over the next few weeks there was a pattern of strange occurrences. She heard the clicking of the light switches as the lights switched themselves on and off with no one near them.

She could also smell rotten eggs, although others in the house could not.

Her then partner did not believe in the supernatural at all until he heard an unexplained noise on one of the doors, like someone drumming their fingers on the wood.

Lesley also found that the temperature in the house seemed to fluctuate violently for no apparent reason.

She was aware that some of the neighbours had had strange experiences too. One lady described seeing the figure of a woman in her hallway on a number of occasions and, when Lesley investigated further, a medium suggested it might be the spirit of her grandmother.

On the Move

Lesley then moved to a house in St Thomas Crescent. These houses had been built before World War II on land that had previously been part of the grounds of Arbroath Abbey.

Her first encounter with the paranormal in her new home came when she came downstairs one morning to find that all of her ornaments had been neatly laid on their sides. Some had been sitting on high shelves, certainly out of reach of her toddler son who was quickly discounted as a possible culprit.

Her partner was 'freaked' by this incident, although what was to follow was even more bizarre.

At the top of the internal stair Lesley had a three-legged table with a pot plant sitting on it. On a number of occasions there would be a great crash. The first time, thinking that their three-year-old had fallen downstairs, the couple ran to the scene to find the table lying in two parts, top and legs, at the foot of the stairs.

What was even stranger was that the plant was sitting upright at the top of the stairs, as if someone had set it down.

Again, their son could not be blamed as sometimes this happened when he was not even in the house.

Lesley points out that the table couldn't have got to the foot of the stairs on its own, particularly as the plant was always left sitting at the top of the stairs.

If that seemed strange what happened next was even more unlikely. Just as they were going out the table fell to the bottom of the stairs, again leaving the plant sitting in place. As the couple were in a rush they decided to leave everything where it was and join the legs and top and take the restored table back to its normal place when they returned. They returned from their outing only to find the table, intact, back at the top of the stairs.

Lying in bed late one night, the couple were awakened by a loud noise. Lesley says it was being like someone dragging a heavy piece of furniture over the floor. (Her partner described it as sounding like a lion roaring – a frightening thought in the middle of Arbroath.)

Lesley says no explanation for the noise was ever found. All of her neighbours were elderly and unlikely to be moving furniture about in the middle of the night.

Another of Lesley's experiences occurred during the night. This time it was the noise of the glass door banging against the window ledge behind it. This had happened with enough force to leave paint chippings on the floor. Describing the situation to me, Lesley pointed out that the door was fitted with a lever handle and was properly closed so draughts or wind could be discounted. Nevertheless this sometime happened four or five times per week.

The couple had a pitbull dog and during one incident it sat growling and staring at the kitchen door but wouldn't go in. Strangely enough, Lesley's cat has shown similar behaviour, often staring at the kitchen or living room doors and even arching its back, showing its teeth and claws as if threatened by something, before whatever it sees frightens it so much that it bolts.

An Unwanted Visitor

It is not just Lesley and her partner who have had odd experiences in the house. Lesley describes finding her young son crying at his bedroom door. He was pointing into the room while crying that he wanted the man to go. Asked to point to the spot he gestured towards the room.

Lesley ordered whoever was there to leave and this seemed to resolve the matter in the short term, although the toddler still said he was scared of the man.

His mother has also heard him talking to his friend although that might be the imaginary friend lots of children have.

On another occasion, Lesley, heavily pregnant and alone in the house, was lying on the bed with her eyes closed although she says she wasn't asleep.

Suddenly, she heard a voice calling "Lesley". Her name was repeated three times in all in a voice that she described as "an evil sounding voice – not at all nice".

Unsurprisingly, she felt she had to get out of the room but found she had to struggle against an invisible force that seemed determined to prevent her leaving.

Once she was out of the room the force disappeared and she found she could move quite freely again.

Lesley says that this was a particularly frightening experience for her. As she had no telephone or transport she was forced to stay in the flat but if she had been able to leave she would have done so.

At Lesley's present house there was little unexplained activity for the first few years she was there but the last couple of years has seen an increase in strange happenings.

As she and a female friend stood in the hallway one day the glass door slammed shut separating the two of them. This particularly alarmed her friend. Again there was no apparent external force, the door just seemed to swing shut on its own

One evening, Lesley was sitting chatting with her Mum and a friend about Lesley's Gran, who had died not long before.

Suddenly, a black ball swooped down from nowhere making Lesley and her friend duck to get out of its way. Her Mum however saw nothing.

Lesley says the black object appears a lot and sometimes travels along the floor.

Perhaps though, the strangest of Lesley's tales concerns her son Ben. He kept talking about Aggie whom she assumed was just an imaginary friend who featured regularly in his conversations at home and even in the car.

One evening, Ben came downstairs crying, saying that Aggie's dog had broken his toys. He described a big black dog with blood streaming down one side of its face.

On another occasion, he announced, "Aggie could swim, he just choked but it's alright now. He sometimes takes me fishing".

While playing on the kitchen floor one day he told his Mum that Aggie was at the door and asked if she could let him in. "Aggie says put the kettle on, he wants a cup of coffee."

When Lesley told Ben's father about Aggie and the various stories about him he turned white.

His father had had a big black Labrador which a friend had accidentally shot in the eye.

He also told Lesley, who had never met his father and knew little about him, that when he went to people's houses he invariably asked for a cup of coffee – and, he had drowned in a boating accident!

Did the little boy have conversations with the grandfather he had never met? Who can say?

Arbroath Abbey

Arbroath Abbey was a very important part of the history of Scotland from the time it was founded in 1178 by King William the Lion until the Scottish Reformation in 1560 (**19**).

It was dedicated to Thomas Becket, chancellor to the English King Henry II, and later Archbishop of Canterbury. Relations between Henry and Becket deteriorated until the King remarked casually, "Will no one rid me of this turbulent priest". Four of Henry's knights took him at his word and murdered Becket in Canterbury Cathedral on December 29th 1170.

Becket's death, effectively at the hands of Henry, meant that he was seen as a martyr and in 1173, he was made St Thomas.

Many miracles were attributed to his intervention. In July 1174, Henry returned from Normandy to deal with a Scottish invasion of England. It is thought that he genuinely regretted Becket's death and he went first to Canterbury Cathedral where he did penance at the martyr's tomb. The effect appeared to be immediate.

Even as Henry left the Cathedral, word came to him that the Scottish King, William, had been captured at Alnwick. The message to both monarchs was obvious and William also decided to take St Thomas's memory very seriously indeed.

After his release, William instructed that a monastery, dedicated to the St Thomas, be built 'near the mouth of the Brothock Burn'.

While William may have indeed wanted to placate St Thomas he was also likely to have seen the dedication of the Abbey to the martyr as an opportunity to add to Henry's guilt.

From its institution, the Abbey played an important part in the history of Scotland.

19 *Arbroath Abbey; hosts singing and chanting monks.*

No more so than in April 1320 when the Declaration of Arbroath, the letter sent to the Pope by the Scottish nobility seeking his backing in the country's struggle to be free of English interference, was apparently signed there.

Some scholars take the view that the document may not have been signed at Arbroath, suggesting only that the final draft may have been put together there by the then Abbot, Bernard de Linton.

But, irrespective of whether there was a gathering of nobles at Arbroath to sign and seal the letter, it proved to be one of the most important documents in Scottish history, and it eventually brought the desired response from the Pope whose influence on European affairs was then of such importance.

The language of the deed is some of the most stirring found anywhere with its call to freedom for all Scots:

For, so long as one hundred remain alive, we will never in any degree be subject to the dominion of the English. Since not for glory, riches or honours do we fight but for freedom alone, which no man loses but with his life.

The document went further than merely asking for papal backing however, being also one of the first recorded documents to suggest that a monarch could be removed by his subjects if he failed to carry out their wishes.

In later years, the influence of the Abbots of Arbroath waned and, with them, that of the Abbey itself although its lands remained a source of income even after the Reformation.

Apparitions in the Abbey

At one point in her life, Lesley Martin knew a number of people who worked at the Abbey and, being interested in the supernatural, she was intrigued by the tales they told her, particularly as her own experiences suggested that the area around the Abbey was indeed haunted.

A female visitor to the Abbey was climbing a stone spiral staircase when she stumbled and started to fall backwards. Hands caught her and steadied her to prevent her falling. When she turned to thank the person who had prevented her having a nasty accident she discovered there was no one there.

As one of the female members of staff was walking across the green one morning on her way to unlock the various buildings she saw someone waving to her from one of the doorways.

The hand was quite distinct and, when telling the story later, the lady had no doubt about what she had seen. What made the tale even stranger was that the door the hand had waved from was securely locked, so the hand had appeared through a locked door!

The large double doors at the Abbey are extremely heavy and consequently very difficult to move but as the staff were checking the premises one day the doors banged shut. There was no question of it being the wind – the doors are too heavy to be moved in that way.

Paranormal investigations have suggested that a ley line, an imaginary line believed to have scientific or even magic properties which connect prehistoric sites, runs directly through the high altar.

This theory could be correct as it is not unusual for Christian churches to be built on sites previously used for pagan worship. It has also been claimed that the high altar site had been used for human sacrifices at some point in the past.

This may have resulted in a break or interruption in the ley line which has been put forward as a theory as to why the Abbey never really prospered.

Apparently, the new visitor centre should not be affected by this and so should experience no such difficulties.

Whether the theory regarding a ley line has any basis in fact the Abbey does seem to harbour some paranormal secrets and it is not just Lesley Martin who has stories of strange goings on at the old Abbey of Aberbrothock.

More Staff Stories

Many of the tales come from former members of the staff themselves.

A male member of the staff saw what appeared to be lights burning in the Abbot's House. He was aware that there should not be anyone in the building and, fearing vandals or other intruders, he went to investigate. When he got there he could find no trace of any intruder but, just as he was leaving, he could clearly hear the sound of monks singing and chanting.

A similar tale is told by another member of staff who was locking up in the Abbot's house when he heard a loud bang from the floor above. Whatever caused the noise also made the building itself shake.

He also thought that there might be vandals in the property and went to investigate. Like his colleague, he made a thorough search but could find no trace of any living individual.

As happens in many of the places prone to paranormal occurrences, sometimes it is the more spiritually perceptive visitor who senses good or bad vibes and one visitor to the Abbey had such an experience a few years ago.

She reported having had a bad feeling about the area close to the Abbot's House. In fact, such was the strength of her intuition that she had had to run out of the building. This seemed surprising, not least of all because one would expect an ecclesiastical building to be a haven of peace rather than a place of evil.

It was only after some thought that staff recalled that that particular area had been the site of the Battle of Arbroath where 600 men were slain in 1446.

Another member of staff was engaged in cleaning when something happened which caused her to swear.

No sooner was the word out of her mouth than she was struck quite forcibly from behind – punishment, she later decided, for blaspheming in a sacred place.

> Arbroath Abbey is open to the public. For details telephone 01241 878756 or consult the website <www.historic-scotland.gov.uk>.

Animal Awareness

One morning during the mid 1980s, a teenage girl was out with her friend and her friend's dogs, walking along behind the houses near the railway line at Cairnie in Arbroath.

Suddenly, apparently out of nowhere, a woman appeared, dressed in a long white, Victorian period dress and carrying a parasol. Trotting along beside her was a dog on a lead.

The vision was there for just a few seconds before disappearing as quickly as it had come.

As one might imagine, the girl and her friend were speechless but to this day she is convinced that she had an encounter with a spirit as there seems to be no other explanation.

The lady gave me no indication as to whether her friend's dogs reacted in any way but, as we have seen, often animals seem to be more perceptive than humans.

A Ferryden lady was out walking her dog towards Scurdieness lighthouse when her dog growled and raised its hackles, as if concerned about something or someone.

She mentioned the incident to her sister whom, it turned out, had had a similar experience with her own dog at exactly the same spot.

I have also had a similar experience when walking my dog over part of the former Montrose airfield one night just as darkness was falling. We had continued to walk on from the seventh hole on the Medal golf course out towards the old .303 rifle range when the dog suddenly stopped and refused to go any further.

Despite my attempts to get her to go forward she flatly refused, although she was quite happy to go back the way we had come.

St Vigeans

OS Map, sheet 54: 639429

The tiny hamlet of St Vigeans just over a mile from Arbroath is dominated by the pre-Reformation church which stands on a grassy mound overlooking the tiny red sandstone cottages.

There had been Christian activity in the area long before the founding of Arbroath Abbey, probably from as long ago as the 6th or 7th century. Little is known of the early church at St Vigeans but there was certainly a church building there by the early part of the 12th century.

The church is dedicated to St Vigean, which comes from Vigianus, the Latin name of the Irish saint Fechin who died in 664. There is no indication that the Saint himself ever came to the area but his followers probably settled there as missionaries some time after his death.

The 12th-century church, part of which is still visible today, was consecrated by Bishop David de Bernham in 1242 and reconsecrated in 1485.

After the Reformation of 1560 the altar was removed and a pulpit installed in line with Protestant style of worship.

For a short time around the time of the Restoration in 1660 the church was used for Episcopalian worship by the Rev Patrick Strachan. His son George attempted to continue the practice but the local Presbytery refused to accept him and normal service was literally resumed.

The church was extended and refurbished in the early 1870s and has since remained largely unaltered.

But local legend treats the history of the church at St Vigeans very differently.

In the supernatural tales of Scotland, the kelpie or water-kelpie, is a being which often takes the form of a horse although it can, for its own dark purposes, transform itself into a handsome young man.

The kelpie is generally found beside a ford or fast flowing stream where it tries to lure the unwary to their doom. In the form of a horse it will be seen feeding beside the river bank, almost inviting any passing traveller to mount it and pass through the water in relative safety.

In fact, nothing could be further from the truth. Having taken its rider half way across it tosses the unfortunate passenger into the air leaving him to drown.

Generally, the kelpie takes the form of a black horse, recognisable by its wild and staring eyes, although there have been instances of the kelpie appearing as a magnificent white stallion.

In its other guise, as a fine looking human, it sets out to try to seduce any member of the fairer sex who happens to be passing. Sometimes, according to the folktales, the young lady recognises the danger she is in only when she spots a fragment of seaweed or perhaps a reed in the young man's hair, showing that he is in fact a creature of the water.

When in equine form it was thought possible for a human to capture a kelpie by throwing a bridle marked with a cross over his head. Once captured, the kelpie could be used for heavy work such as carrying heavy stones for the erection of farm buildings.

One thing was certain about the kelpie however – at the first opportunity it would make its escape.

For years, many of the local people believed that the church at St Vigeans had been built over a large, underground loch, supported on a series of large iron bars.

Added to that was the fact that they also believed that a captured kelpie had been put to work to carry the stones to build the kirk and that the use of a supernatural being for such purposes would bring with it its own dangers.

According to the legend, the kelpie had prophesied that one of the ministers at St Vigeans would commit suicide and that, at the first communion celebrated afterwards, the church would sink into the loch underneath.

When the first part of the prophecy came true there were, understandably, fears about the safety of the building and from 1699 until 1736 no communion services were held there.

In that year, it was decided to celebrate communion but large numbers of the population, fearing that both church and congregation would sink into the bowels of the earth, watched from a safe distance.

The Kirk, and those brave enough to take part in the service, all survived the experience.

The Morphie Kelpie

This was another instance of a kelpie being used to carry stones for a building, although this one took place in the county of Kincardine-shire, just north of Montrose.

The Grahams of Morphie were one of the most powerful families in the area and also owned the lands of Charleton.

One of the old lairds is reputed to have captured a kelpie in the time-honoured fashion using a bridle. Some sources refer to it as a pair of branks, a term more generally associated with a method of punishment used on witches or nagging women, but in fact it can also mean a bridle with wooden sides.

Anyway, having caught his prey, the laird used the kelpie to drag the heavy stones he needed to the site where he was building his castle. After the castle was completed the kelpie either escaped or was given its freedom.

The kelpie apparently felt ill used because of the arduous nature of the work he had been forced to carry out and as he headed towards the River North Esk he was heard to curse the laird by uttering the following rhyme:

> Sair back and sair banes, [bones]
> Drivin' the laird o' Morphies stanes! [stones]
> The laird o' Morphie 'll never thrive
> As lang's the kelpy is alive!

The curse caused the male line of the Graham family to die out so it might be said that the kelpie had the last laugh.

The Lost Piper

Just north of Arbroath on the A92 to Montrose is the farm of Dickmontlaw which has associations with a tragedy. A piper, by the name of Tom Tyrie, was, according to some accounts, returning from a wedding with his wife and dog, when they took shelter in the Forbidden Cave near the town.

After the festivities, the pair were probably somewhat the worse for drink and, unable to find their way out, they were believed to have starved to death in the darkness.

Their dog is reputed to have escaped but the piper and his wife were never seen again.

Tom's spirit is still said to be seeking the way out and he can sometimes be heard playing as he continues his fruitless search for the open air.

According to some versions, the music is said to come from the hearth of the old farmhouse of Dickmontlaw which is several miles from the coast and was destroyed by fire a number of years ago.

Often, similar ghost stories are told as having happened at some other location and this is one of those occasions.

Lauriston Castle is the site of a number of tunnels, leading from the castle down to the shore. A blind piper, accompanied by his dog, is reputed to have wandered into one of the tunnels and eventually found himself in the castle's cellar. He could be heard beneath the castle playing his pipes but, according to one version of the story, the laird was away from home and had taken the cellar key with him.

So the unfortunate piper was doomed to death in the cellar and his playing became less and less frequent although it is said that he can still be heard on occasions playing a lament in recognition of his sorry situation.

Legend has it that the Laird of Lauriston hears the piper only once – on the night before his own death!

Edzell Castle

Sometime in the early part of the 14th century the wife of a serf in the barony of Edzell gave birth to twins.

Nothing unusual about that, although the twins themselves appear to have been different from their fellows. Their father had died just a few months earlier leaving his wife, who was reputed to be of gypsy stock, to bring up the two boys on her own.

One of the boys had a large red spot on his left cheek and some spots on his hip and back while the other had spots on his brow, nose and chin.

The physical marks might have been enough to make them outcasts but, as they got older, it became obvious that they had no language, although otherwise they were full of life and energy.

Their mother took offence if anyone mentioned their disability however, few, if any did, mainly because most of the neighbours were afraid of her. Knowing of her supposed gypsy background they were convinced that she possessed supernatural powers.

Even the Laird, Lord Crawford, treated the family with great consideration, showering them with gifts and other favours.

The boys grew up to be strong, hardy young men with few equals in physical activities such as running, jumping or wrestling. They were also expert hunters, although they never hunted with any of the other men from the estate.

The fact that they shunned the company of others made them appear more mysterious and the local people thought that the twins, like their mother, had supernatural powers, a belief that their mother actively encouraged.

A Hunting Party

All of this took place in the reign of Robert the Bruce, Scotland's warrior King. Wolves were killing many of the King's sheep and the King decided that they must be hunted down and killed.

He called upon all the landed men of the area to assemble at the Castle of Menmuir, along with their wolf hounds and beagles and 20 of their best men.

Crawford, like the rest of the landowners, wanted to impress the King and after considerable thought he decided, with reservations, to include the twins, of whose hunting skills there could be no doubt, in his hunting party.

Each party was allocated a section of the forest and set off to search for their prey.

Contact was soon made with seven wolves and, after a chase, the wolves were finally cornered by seven wolf dogs.

The hunters were some way behind with the twins ahead of their fellows. Unlike the other hunters, neither twin had a spear, although each was armed with a large hunting knife and carried a large sack.

The other hunters could hear rustling from inside the bags but, in view of the twins' reputation, asked no questions.

No matter which way the wolves tried to escape their passage was blocked by either men or dogs.

Initially, the dogs were sent to deal with the ferocious animals but they were quickly killed by the desperate wolves.

20 *Edzell Castle; where a thief got more than he bargained for.*

Just as the leaders were considering a full scale attack the twins rushed forward ahead of their fellows. Each opened his sack to release a total of seven hawks. The birds each flew towards an individual wolf and, fixing their talons on their prey's neck, pecked out the eyes leaving the wolf blind.

Once the hawks had done their work the twins rushed forward and soon dispatched the now blind wolves by cutting their throats with their hunting knives.

None of the other groups had killed as many wolves so the party from Edzell were declared champions of the day.

A Grudging Respect

To show his gratitude, Crawford bestowed further favours on the twins and their mother, even building them a fine cottage on the estate.

He also appointed the twins to supply fish, venison and game for the castle table. Behind it all however, he was still afraid of the family and their apparently supernatural powers.

On the surface, everything seemed to be fine. His Lordship wanted for nothing as far as food supplies from the rivers and forests were concerned.

There were rumours however that the twins were engaging in private trade involving Lord Crawford's deer and sheep. Crawford was unwilling to listen to the stories but, eventually, he could not ignore the tales any longer and he sent men out to secretly watch the pair at work.

The twins seemed to know that they were being spied upon but, although the watchers saw nothing amiss, the numbers of deer and sheep on the estate continued to diminish.

One evening, there was a huge celebration at the castle with food and wine in abundance. It was noted that the twins were not present. Men were set to watch the family cottage and they saw the twins arrive with a fine stag they had killed.

The men rushed the twins and, after a momentous struggle, eventually managed to overwhelm them.

Justice was swift in those days and they were brought to trial before Lord Crawford the following morning. Even allowing for their disability the two made no attempt to deny the charge by sign or other means and, having been caught red-handed, were sentenced to hang.

As the sentence was about to be carried out, their mother appeared. She looked up to where Lord and Lady Crawford were watching from the Castle windows and shouted:

> "By all the demons of Hell! I curse you! Lady Crawford, you shall not see the sun set; you, and the unborn babe you carry will both be buried in the same grave; and for you Lord Crawford, you shall die a death that would make the boldest man ever born of woman, even to witness, shriek with fear."

Crawford called to his men to arrest her but she was gone and, despite a search of the forest, no trace was ever found of her.

The Mother's Curse

According to legend, Lady Crawford took ill that very day and her baby, born prematurely, was stillborn. Just as the gypsy woman had predicted, the two were buried in the same grave.

Crawford mourned for 18 months before marrying a rich and beautiful woman.

The wedding celebrations were a lavish affair lasting over a week. As was common in those days a great hunt was organised and a large number of knights and their ladies took part.

At around mid-day on a fine autumn day, the hunting party saw a fine stag and gave chase until it was eventually cornered at the very spot where the wolves had been killed.

It was quickly killed and the servants cut up its body as Lord Crawford no doubt congratulated himself on a fine day's sport for himself and his guests.

Suddenly, two large wolves appeared apparently out of nowhere and leapt at Crawford, dragging him from the saddle. Within minutes he had been torn apart and the wolves disappeared as quickly and silently as they had appeared.

Those who saw the deed, and indeed all who heard of it, believed that the two wolves embodied the spirit of the twins who had returned to take a dreadful revenge.

The oak tree from which the twins had been hanged survived until the 16th century but the locals swore that on dark stormy nights the ghosts of the twins could be seen below its branches, making signs with their hands and howling unintelligible threats in the wind.

Photographic Evidence

On the 3rd of March 1993, the *Montrose Review* carried a story about the ghost of Edzell Castle on its front page. The story was illustrated by a picture of the Castle taken by Carole Rollman, a photographer at the nearby United States Navy communications base at what was formerly RAF Edzell.

Ms Rollman's picture appeared to capture a figure dressed in black, standing at a window. There is no floor behind the window so it would be impossible for anyone to be there.

It has been suggested that early shrouds were black, hence the black figure in the photograph, although that does not really tie in with the fact that the spirit regularly seen in the grounds is known as the White Lady, believed to be Catherine Campbell, the wife of David Lindsay, the ninth Earl of Southesk.

Catherine was an epileptic who, according to legend, lapsed into unconsciousness during the winter of 1543. She stayed in a coma for several days and was eventually declared dead.

Her body was then wrapped in a shroud and bedecked in precious jewels, an action that did in fact bring about her death. The supposed corpse was carried about 400 yards to the family vault in Edzell Cemetery where it was laid out on a stone slab to await burial the following day. The lure of the precious stones was too much for the sexton who decided that he would steal her jewellery. Under the cover of darkness he made his way to where her body had been laid and began the grisly work of removing the jewellery.

He was unable however to prise the rings from her swollen hands and decided that the simplest solution was to cut her fingers off. As he set about his gruesome task the body is said to have moved and called out, "Alas".

Possibly grateful for the fact that the sexton's evil actions had made her regain consciousness Lady Lindsay is reputed to have forgiven the rascal and allowed him to keep his ill-gotten gains.

She returned to the gate of the Castle where the guards, faced with the figure of someone they believed to be dead, refused to let her in. Forced to stay outside in the cold, the poor woman died of exposure.

The sexton did not profit from his evil doings either, as he was captured and hanged.

At the time of Ms Rollman's picture, the curator was Geoff Hutson. He is a believer and was willing to relate his story to me.

> "During my time at the Castle I had the good fortune to encounter the White Lady many times. I say this because I never felt any feeling of evil or unease.
>
> Most happenings took place in the garden. She would come through the wall just up from the bathhouse door, cross the hedge-lawn and then go through the wall at the north-east side of the Tower House.
>
> Every time she appeared, a heavy scent, hard to put into a type, filled the air.
>
> On two occasions she appeared mid afternoon in front of the Tower house entrance. The other place that I have caught sight of her at different times of the day was in the kitchen/store next to the Tower.
>
> Only once did I ever see her at the Lindsay Vault and that was at midday. She was still there up until 1994 at least."

A Lost Love

Another tale of a ghost at Edzell Castle came from an American serviceman who was stationed at the US base.

He admitted to having a fascination for history and decided to tour the Castle. Then, there were no guides so visitors were free to explore the site as they pleased. As he wandered through a part of the building he felt an odd sensation, as if someone was running their fingers through his hair.

It was beginning to get dark and, suddenly, the air felt distinctly cooler so, perhaps unsurprisingly, the young American decided it was time to take his leave of Edzell Castle.

As he passed through the garden gate he was brought crashing to the ground. He was convinced that he did not stumble or fall over his own feet so he could only conclude that he had been tripped but, when he looked around, there was no one else there.

The following day, he told his strange story to Mrs Betty Morton, then the Community Adviser at the Base. A local woman, she was able to give him a ghostly explanation of his experience.

According to local legend, the Lindsays were Episcopalians and a daughter of the family had fallen in love with a young Presbyterian boy.

The girl's father discovered that the pair were having secret trysts but such were the religious tensions of the period that even the possibility of a mixed marriage enraged the girl's father. As result, he forbade her to continue with the meetings but, needless to say, the young couple continued to see each other.

Suspecting as much, the father hid himself outside the gate one night and waited for his daughter's lover to make his way home from the Castle. As the unfortunate youth passed by, the father tripped him up and murdered him.

The daughter, totally distraught at the loss of her lover, never recovered and soon died of a broken heart.

Legend has it that the daughter's ghost still haunts the Castle searching for her lost love. She is reputed to be particularly fond of young male visitors and 'welcomes' them by running her fingers through their hair.

Having had this treatment, the young American could only conclude that her father had been waiting for him at the gate to trip him up!

One young man, whose grandfather was the gardener at Edzell, is in no doubt about the existence of the ghost.

One afternoon, he and his grandmother took grand-dad a cup of tea. It was a lovely day and they all sat and chatted in the sunhouse until after 5pm.

As he and his Granny were making their way home they saw the ghost. Asked what happened next he answered truthfully – "We ran like hell!"

Telephone 01356 648631 or consult <www.historic-scotland.gov.uk>.

Ghosts on the Road

The road around Muirdrum is reputed to be haunted by a number of spirits of various types.

Muriel Mc...... recalled hearing the tale of a horseman, frequently seen near the old wood at the top of Carlogie Road, who would gallop off in the general direction of the Forfar Road.

There are other stories of a young woman, another vision known as the White Lady, who walks along the roadside near Muirdrum. She used to make her appearances in the dip in the old road just as you turn off from Muirdrum to Carnoustie.

The area has been completely changed by the development of the dual carriageway so it may be that she has had to find pastures new or perhaps she still patrols the line of the old road seeking to upset travellers from a different age.

There are further tales of another spirit that walks the main road close to Arbroath. It is also the figure of a woman but those who get close to her find that her face shines brightly, as if lit by some paranormal means.

A Fairy Story

Close to Muirdrum lies the area known as Balmachie. One day many years ago, the Laird of Balmachie left his estate to travel to Dundee to transact some business there. His wife was ill so he left her behind in the care of a neighbour.

After completing his business, the Laird returned by a slightly different route, leaving the main road and travelling across country, through the area known as Carlungie.

As he rode along, he became aware of a group of little people dragging behind them a litter bearing the form of a human.

Now the Laird was a man of considerable courage and, while others might have looked the other way and ridden on, he drew his sword and rode up to the procession. There, he demanded that the fairies, for that is what they were, release their prisoner.

The little people dropped their human cargo and disappeared. When the Laird looked more closely at the figure on the litter he was astonished to find that it was his own wife, dressed in her nightclothes, just as he had left her.

He wrapped his cloak around her and helped her onto his horse and the pair made their way back to their home.

Once safely indoors, he carried his wife to another room where he left her to be cared for by his neighbour.

He then went to the bedroom where he had left his wife earlier that day. There, in the bed, lay what appeared to be his sick wife.

The figure was most unhappy, complaining about his absence and saying that she was stiff with cold.

Apparently showing great concern, the Laird had a fire lit in the room and suggested she come and sit by it in the warmth. The figure protested that she was too ill and weak to move but the Laird picked her up and carried her towards the fireplace. Instead of placing her on the fireside chair however, he suddenly threw the figure into the flames.

The figure did not linger in the fire for more than a fraction of a second, flying upwards through the roof leaving only a hole as evidence of a supernatural presence.

Now that she was safe, the Laird brought his wife from the other room, through into the warmth where she told him what had happened after he had left that morning.

When the neighbour had left her briefly to go about some household task, a group of fairies had come into the room and carried her out through the window. After that, she could remember nothing until her husband had appeared to rescue her from their clutches.

The hole in the roof was soon mended but, no matter how well the repair was carried out, each year, on the anniversary of the incident, the hole would reappear at the very same spot.

Activity in Carnoustie

Donald Cunningham lived in a large Victorian house in Philip Street in Carnoustie but from his early childhood he felt insecure in the house, particularly in two of the rooms. Even as a young adult he admitted the house caused him serious concerns.

On the landing halfway up the stairs was a bureau with a plastic model football on it. Donald was in the bathroom one day when he heard a loud crash. The ball had struck his parents' bedroom door with some force and was now lying at the foot of the door. There was no logical explanation for what had happened.

When he went to bed that night he could hear what he described as an 'ungodly' voice saying, "This is my house". The words were always repeated twice.

Donald kept piles of small change on his bedside cabinet and, in the morning each pile was sitting at a 45° angle. Again, there was no explanation for this strange phenomenon.

A local minister was asked to visit and he and a colleague blessed every corner of the house.

The minister felt that the house itself was 'shrouded in darkness' and he therefore encouraged a happier feeling. To facilitate this, he suggested that doors, cupboards and drawers should be left open for easy access. He thought too that children's toys had been locked away for too long and he recommended unpacking some and leaving them lying around.

Not long after the blessing had taken place, Donald became aware of a bright light filling the upper part of the house. Even a dark little living room appeared to be bathed in light and the table lamps appeared to give off more light than they had before.

The light may only have been sunlight but Donald was unaware of such an effect before.

Donald investigated the history of the house which had originally been owned by a wealthy jute baron. After that it had been rented out to a succession of tenants but Donald's family had lived there for 40 years.

Strangely enough, Donald later discovered that a neighbour had had a similar experience. His children refused to sleep in one of the rooms as the bedcovers were regularly pulled off the bed by unseen forces.

Since leaving the family home Donald has lived in three other properties but has had no further strange experiences.

A Nose for Spirits

Many of those I interviewed talked of experiencing strange smells which couldn't be readily explained and this is an example.

Ron and Barbara Gray bought a building plot in Carnoustie which had originally been part of an orchard.

Obviously, the first part of the work involved digging out foundations and during that phase of the work, a number of pieces of clay pipes, of the smoking variety, were found.

The couple thought little of that until the house was completed some three years later.

Shortly afterwards, Ron came in from work one day and smelt pipe tobacco in the downstairs hallway.

He asked Barbara if she had had any visitors but there had been no one else in the house that day and he says she is definitely not a pipe smoker!

During the next four years both Ron and Barbara regularly smelt their 'visitor', usually under the open staircase in the entrance hallway, although Barbara caught a whiff of the distinctive smell between the lounge and the dining room on at least one occasion.

Again, they could find no explanation for these strange experiences.

Strange Happenings

Not all paranormal incidents concern ghosts or fairies. A few years ago, schoolteacher Dennis Arnot and a friend were walking back from Glen Tannar to Tarfside. It was a dark night, so dark that they literally couldn't see their hands in front of their faces.

Suddenly, they became aware of a group of small lights somewhere in the distance.

There were four or five points of light that moved, sometimes slowly and sometimes much faster. They would rise up into the air and then fall down again, while at other times they would dart from left to right and then back again

At times they disappeared from view altogether before reappearing to give another brief light show.

Dennis could find no explanation then and, even now, can give no logical explanation as to what the lights were or what caused them.

Mysterious lights in the sky are, of course, nothing new. Lots of people believe in unidentified flying objects and conspiracy theories, usually that governments are aware of such things but won't admit it, abound.

Certainly, we now understand that the universe is so vast that it is perfectly possible that life of some sort may exist elsewhere, although whether such life forms would have the advanced technology required to travel immense distance through space is another matter.

If we are being watched by superior intelligences it would appear reasonable that they would take a particular interest in the human race when we develop what are, to us at any rate, new technologies.

It was with that thought in mind that I searched the local press for UFO sightings after the setting up of the aerodrome at Montrose in 1913.

I was not disappointed. There, in the *Montrose Review* dated 7th March 1913, just days after the arrival of the Royal Flying Corps at Dysart, was an article headed 'The Airship Scares' which described how members of the public had reported seeing strange lights in the sky.

> What was supposed to be the mysterious airship was seen from Craigo village on Sabbath night by a number of people. About 9.00pm a glow of light of a red and white colour was observed hovering over Glenskenno Wood on the Craigo estate.
>
> The light then took a northerly course for some distance and finally going slowly in a north-west direction it disappeared.
>
> The weather was somewhat foggy, but the light could be distinctly seen moving in the directions stated.
>
> As seen from the village, the light did not seem to be very high in the air. On Thursday night, about 10.00pm, a light of the same description was seen floating in much the same direction as that on Sabbath night.

As the earlier remarks on the setting up of the Montrose air station make clear there was concern about German airships flying into British air space on spying missions. This seems to have been well known and the problem appears to have been a matter of considerable public disquiet.

The *Review* suggested that the sky watchers were no doubt sincere and, while they had undoubtedly seen lights, it did not follow that these were airships and, even if they were, certainly not that they were German.

It was even suggested that sightings of the planets Mars or Venus might be more plausible explanations but, of course, planets do not appear to move any distance over such a short space of time.

The *Review* itself discounted the idea of spies from above, pointing out that foreign airships had no need to show lights and, because of their secret mission, would not do so anyway.

Night flying from Dysart can also be discounted. No 2 Squadron spent the first few weeks of their time at Montrose flying over the area to familiarise themselves with the terrain. The idea that some would have flown over the area within days of their arrival, particularly on a foggy night, seems a step too far even for the intrepid aviators of the RFC.

So we are left with the choice of an airship, British or foreign, or an alien flying machine investigating our capabilities.

Common sense would suggest an airship but ...... !

Reporting a Death?

Another strange happening involving the military concerned a soldier from Montrose who took part in the First World War.

Charles Bowman had been a star player for the local football team before his search for work took him south of the border.

In the spring of 1915, by which time he was aged 36 and had three children with his wife Lizzie, he decided to do his patriotic duty and enlist in the Gordon Highlanders.

He was posted to Aberdeen and his family came to live in the Granite City. In late June of 1916, with her husband posted to France, Lizzie came to stay with relatives in Montrose.

Bowman was killed in the Battle of the Somme on 18th August 1916. The story of Charles Bowman is a tragic one, like that of so many others who fought in the same conflict.

In this case though, there is a strange postscript, told later by Bowman's niece Mary.

The house in Montrose was on three levels, with an outside door and a short hallway leading to a glass door where visitors normally knocked or rang to announce their presence. On the ground floor there were a number of rooms and a stair to the next floor and then another short stair from the first floor that led to the attic. The bathroom was directly opposite the top of the first stair.

The family were having a meal in the kitchen when they heard the sound of heavy footsteps coming in the front door, then moving along the passage before climbing the stair and going into the bathroom. One of the family went to confront the 'intruder' but there was no one else in the house. Lizzie announced, "That's a warning".

Although nobody thought to note the date and time of this bizarre event Mary believed "it was about that time that Uncle Charlie was killed in France".

In another strange incident, one of the pilots who had been initially based at Montrose was shot down during WWI, although he was uninjured. He appeared to his mother on the stairs of their home as a sign that he was still alive.

Bad Luck!

There are those moments where it is difficult if not impossible to decide where someone has just been lucky or whether fate or a guardian angel, call it what you will, decides to intervene.

One such instance was the case of Montrose artist and potter Syd Walker. Back in the 1960s, Syd worked from a pottery in Bridge Street in Montrose, across the street from the Public Library.

At the time, he had a gas kiln that required quite a bit of work. Everything had to be stacked into it and then the fire bricks had to be built up round about the items to be fired. Even then, it was extremely slow in getting up to the right temperature.

As a result, it was often the case that he would have the kiln on during the day and then have to return to the pottery in the evening to switch it off.

One evening in May 1968, he was preparing to do exactly that. He had just left the house with his elder daughter Fiona when a television programme came on describing a new, foolproof procedure for attaching handles to cups.

Realising that Syd would be interested, his wife Elizabeth knocked on the window to him and the pair came back and watched the programme. Once it was over, the two set off again for the pottery.

Elizabeth went to make a telephone call from the house. The main instrument was in the pottery and she had just started on her call when the line went dead.

Just minutes later, the telephone in the house rang. It was Syd, calling from one of the houses next to the pottery. He asked her to sit down and the news he gave her was a shock.

A lorry carrying five tons of steel had struck one of the bollards beside the Library before jack-knifing and careering into the pottery. Anyone inside would have been killed.

As it was, it had narrowly missed the hairdressers next door. Another few inches to the side and there would undoubtedly have been casualties, if not fatalities.

By the time Syd and Fiona arrived at the pottery the lorry had already crashed into the building but had they not stopped to watch the item on television they would have been inside, with the likelihood that one or both would have been killed.

The question is, was the delay just good fortune or was some unseen hand at work to delay Syd and Fiona's arrival at the accident scene?

One neighbour had no doubts about the situation. Among the stock Syd had on show were Japanese parasols, one of which had been put up for display in the shop window. Her view of the cause of the accident was quite simple – everyone knows it is bad luck to put an umbrella up indoors!

Tales of the Glens

The Angus Glens are home to numerous tales of the supernatural.

During the early part of the 19th century, the Rev. John Row was minister of Navar and Lethnot.

Just a few minutes walk from the Manse was the miller's house, built of stone and clay with an earth floor and covered by slates from the nearby quarry. By the 1960s it was being used as a hen house and by now it will probably have disappeared altogether.

The miller's name was Black and, like most his fellows, he was reputed to be a quarrelsome individual, although it may just be that millers have had a bad press.

Anyway, Mr Black had fallen out with the farmer from the Wirran, a farm some two miles away down the glen.

Whatever the fall out had been about it was obviously serious, at least as far as Black was concerned, as he planned to ambush the unfortunate farmer as he made his way home in the dark.

The miller's wife was most unhappy about his intentions and she tried every argument to convince her husband that he should stay at home but all of her arguments fell on deaf ears.

As a last resort, she tried tears and asked who would keep her company if she was left on her own. The miller's response was short and to the point, "The devil if he likes".

As readers might guess, the miller's words were prophetic. About two hours after he had left home the figure of Auld Nick himself emerged from the earth floor in a cloud of noxious smoke.

Now the miller's wife obviously had her wits about her. No sooner was the first hint of smoke in her nostrils than she pushed her son out the window and bade him run to the Manse and fetch the Minister.

Luckily, Mr Row was at home and he immediately set off for the miller's house, accompanied by a small group of neighbours who had heard the lad's shouts.

No one really believed the boy's story but as they neared the house the evil smelling fumes that had accompanied the De'il's appearance filled their nostrils.

The Minister quickly realised that he was dealing with a supernatural being and, after a few moments thought, he returned hastily to the Manse. There he dressed in his preaching gown and, picking up his Bible, he set off again for the miller's house.

There, he threw open the door and strode confidently into the room. Faced with the man of God the De'il uttered a fearsome screech before disappearing back into the earth floor.

According to legend, Auld Nick's rapid disappearance left a hollow in the earth floor which was a topic of conversation for visitors for years afterwards.

Tempting Fate

While we cannot fault Mr Row's courage it may have been that even he eventually overreached himself and allowed the Devil to get his revenge.

It was on Christmas Eve 1745 and the Minister, by then in his late sixties, had taken a funeral service for someone who had committed suicide. Despite the reservations of the congregation that suicides should not be buried in consecrated ground, a belief that was widely held in those days, Mr Row insisted on the burial being in the Kirkyard.

The interment had been late in the day and, as darkness began to fall, Mr Row shocked his flock by jumping three times over the open grave to show how silly their superstitious beliefs were.

Thinking no more about it, the Minister returned to his study on the first floor of the Manse. As he sat in the darkening room he became aware of a pair of eyes shining in the dim light.

The eyes belonged to a large black cat and Mr Row would have been well aware that tradition meant that the cat was the De'il himself, 'in shape o' beast', as Robert Burns would later describe a similar situation in Tam o' Shanter.

Mr Row called on his maid servant to fetch a candle and a hay fork and, suitably equipped, he made to drive the cat back to where it had come from.

Standing at the top of the stairs he lunged at the cat with the pitchfork. Perhaps he was over excited by the cat's sudden appearance or just driven on by the adrenalin of the day. Anyway, for whatever reason, he overbalanced and fell over the banister on to the floor beneath and broke his neck.

As ever, it is an interesting tale but even if it has some truth in it the plaque commemorating the Minister makes no mention of how he died.

Strangely enough, the area has another ghost story concerning the miller's brother, James Black, although this spirit is definitely not genuine.

James was a bachelor and farmer who had done extremely well for himself financially.

Close to where he lived, several unfortunate travellers had lost their lives while trying to cross the nearby river while it was in spate. The answer, obviously, was to build a bridge but the question was, who should pay for it?

James was certainly well enough off to afford the cost of building a bridge but could he be convinced to part with the necessary money?

21 *The Tay Rail Bridge; the piers of the original can be clearly seen alongside the current structure.*

A group of his friends decided to give him a ghost experience of his own. On three successive nights he had a visit from the 'ghost' of one of the drowned travellers who pleaded with him to have a bridge built so that no other unfortunates would meet the same fate.

The ruse worked, for not only did James pay the full cost of Gannochy Bridge, which was completed in 1732, but he actually built the parapets himself.

The Tay Bridge Disaster

Dundee has many ghosts, sufficient no doubt for a whole book of its own, but three of the more famous haunted sites are perhaps worthy of mention here.

Few people with any knowledge of modern Scottish history will be unaware of the dreadful tragedy on 28th December 1879 when the Tay Bridge collapsed in a terrible storm (**21**).

The two main railway companies, the Caledonian and the North British were engaged in a struggle for control of the east coast route. If the North British Company was to compete it required a direct rail link to the north but this meant that it was necessary to cross the Rivers Forth and Tay.

Bridging either of those two great rivers was seen as an impossible dream but, to the Victorians, all things were possible, and to Thomas Bouch, very much the Victorian engineer, such dreams were merely challenges to be overcome.

Bouch had proposed bridging the Tay as early as 1854 but the Directors of the Company had labelled the venture 'insane'. Such criticism merely spurred Bouch on to try again.

Apart from the technical difficulties it was obvious to the Directors that a venture like this would incur a huge cost. That said, it was equally obvious that, if the North British Company was to compete with its rival, it had to bridge the rivers and give its passengers a direct, and more importantly, faster route to the north.

It took fifteen years before the shareholders of the North British finally accepted that if they were to gain a commercial advantage then the bridge had to be built. Even then, the money for the venture was raised by a separate company consisting of industrialists and other parties with vested interests in the building of a direct rail link from Edinburgh and, perhaps more importantly, between the coalfields of Fife and the steam powered factories of Dundee!

As all railway building at the time required Parliamentary approval there was much lobbying to be done but, in July 1870, the Bill to erect a bridge over the Tay passed into law and almost a year later work started on Bouch's great project.

Just over six years later the bridge was completed at a total cost of some £300,000 and the first official crossing was made by the relevant dignitaries on 26th September 1877.

Into the Tay

On that fatal night in late December 1879, it was just a few minutes after 7.15pm when a passenger train from the south started to cross the bridge during the worst storm in living memory. It never reached the other side.

The bridge collapsed and the train, along with the 75 unfortunate souls believed to be on board, was lost in the icy waters of the River Tay.

It is tempting to write lost forever but while the passengers and train crew all perished, 46 bodies were later recovered from the deep and the locomotive, No 224, was salvaged, repaired and continued in service for a number of years, known by the ironic nickname of 'the Diver'.

There was, of course, a public inquiry into the disaster and the blame was laid fairly and squarely on engineer Thomas Bouch.

Bouch himself felt that the train may have been derailed and that carriages colliding with the framework of the bridge had caused it to collapse.

The inquiry decided otherwise, with suggestions that the bridge had been poorly designed with no account having been made for the power of the wind.

There were allegations too that the construction methods had been at fault, that the materials used were often of inferior quality and that columns had been cosmetically repaired, each problem adding to the overall weakness of the whole structure.

Even today, books are still being written and new theories explored as to the likely causes of the disaster, although it is probable that the collapse of the bridge was due to a combination of all of these factors, and modern thinking suggests that the wind may have played a more major part in the disaster than previously believed.

The point of the tale from this book's point of view is that just after 7.15pm on the 28th December each year, the anniversary of the disaster, it is said that the lights of a ghost train can be seen crossing the old bridge and that the screams of the passengers can be heard as the 'Diver' and its carriages fall once more into the icy water as the 'bridge' collapses.

Are they perhaps trying to draw attention to their plight and blaming one or all of those they hold responsible?

Chilling Thoughts

The Royal Research Ship *Discovery* was launched in Dundee in 1901 (22). She had been custom built for the use of the British National Antarctic Expedition which, led by Captain Robert Falcon Scott, was to explore that vast icy wilderness.

Scott was then a young and relatively inexperienced Naval Officer but the *Discovery* expedition was the foundation of his reputation as a Polar explorer.

Sadly, his fame is largely as the man who finally reached the South Pole after his rival Amundsen and then died on the return journey. Despite his failure, he was hailed as a hero and awarded a posthumous knighthood.

By the early 1900s, there were few shipyards with the expertise to build a wooden hulled ship capable of withstanding the pressures of being trapped in ice over a long period but the Dundee yards, with their experience of building whaling ships, had retained the necessary skills and knowledge and so got the contract to build this famous ship.

There can be no doubt as to the quality of its construction as its ability to withstand the pressure of the Antarctic ice was proved beyond doubt when it was trapped for two whole winters.

During the expedition, Scott and his party spent their time exploring the continent and adding to the scientific community's knowledge of that alien world.

In the Antarctic summer of 1903-04, two relief ships, *Morning* and the Dundee whaler *Terra Nova*, arrived, charged with either freeing the *Discovery* or, if the worst came to the worst, bringing home the crew and leaving the ship to its icy fate.

The outcome was rather more positive than might have been anticipated as, despite the presence of some 18 miles of solid ice between the *Discovery* and the open sea, they were eventually able to free her.

22 *RRS* Discovery; *may still have an explorer on board.*

One theory is that the *Discovery* was freed due to the knowledge of Dundonian Harry McKay, the captain of the *Terra Nova*, whose experience of using explosives to free whaling ships trapped in the Arctic ice played a significant role in the release of the stricken ship.

Scott himself believed, or may just have wanted to believe, that his ship was freed by the natural sea swell breaking up the ice, aided by the butting of the *Terra Nova* and the other relief ship, the *Morning* and it is that view that has passed into history.

Certainly, if MacKay's part in the relief effort was as important as it seems to have been, he got no credit for it from Scott.

By 14th February 1904, the *Terra Nova's* job was more or less complete and the *Discovery* was free and able to make her way home.

Later, the *Discovery* was sold on to the Hudson Bay Company and, despite Scott's wish to purchase the vessel for his final, fatal expedition, they were not willing to sell her and he had to make do with the *Terra Nova* instead.

The story of the *Discovery* goes full circle however, as she returned to Dundee in the spring of 1986, eventually taking her place at the custom built, Discovery Point, where she serves as a memorial, not just to Scott and the other Antarctic explorers, but also to the men who built her, as well as being a major tourist attraction for her home city.

The Spirit of the *Discovery*

Visitors are sometimes unwilling to go into certain parts of the ship while others hear the sound of unexplained footsteps. Many have seen a shadowy figure but perhaps the most intriguing tale is of a vision so real that a number of visitors have engaged him in conversation without realising that the sailor is a spirit.

One woman is said to have spent a whole evening speaking to him while other people in the same company were unable to see anyone.

During the voyage out to Antarctica, a young sailor called Charles Bonner fell to his death from the rigging and some of the strange happenings are attributed to him.

There is another belief however that the spirit that haunts the *Discovery* is that of another polar explorer, Ernest Shackleton, who was one of the members of the 1901 expedition.

Shackleton was sent home by Scott on the relief vessel *Morning* in March 1903, apparently suffering from scurvy, although there have been suggestions that Scott saw him as a rival, which indeed he was, and so decided to be rid of him at the first opportunity.

Of course, Shackleton went on to have his own career as an explorer, although he never managed to achieve the level of public adulation lavished on Scott.

In 1908-09, he managed to get within 97 miles of the South Pole but was unable to achieve his final goal.

Shackleton's main claim to fame came during his 1914-16 expedition when his ship, the *Endurance*, was crushed by the ice and he led his party to Elephant Island and from there, along with a party of five, successfully traversed over 800 miles of ocean to get help for their stranded companions.

The theory that the spirit might be that of Shackleton stems from the suggestion that he loved the *Discovery* so much that he was unwilling in death to leave her.

Part of this story may be because the electric light bulb over Shackleton's bunk is known to 'blow' frequently. The circuitry has been checked but no technical explanation has been found for this, apparently regular, occurrence.

In fact, Shackleton died of a heart attack in 1922 in South Georgia while preparing for another expedition so it would appear unlikely that his spirit would have come 'home' to the *Discovery* but who can say?

There is of course another possibility. It may be that Harry McKay, having been denied the credit for freeing the *Discovery* in life, has come back to make that very point after his death.

Whatever the truth, and perhaps more than one spirit haunts the ship, it would appear that there is more to the *Discovery* than just being a relic of early 20th century exploration.

HMS *Unicorn*

Another part of Dundee's maritime history is represented by HMS *Unicorn*, the oldest warship afloat having been built at Chatham in 1824.

The *Unicorn* carried 46 guns but was never engaged in active service so no one died on board as a result of enemy action. Rather less romantically, a caretaker is supposed to have died on the vessel when he fell down a set of steps.

Whether the spirit of the unfortunate caretaker continues to haunt the ship we cannot be certain but it is apparently the scene of considerable poltergeist activity. Large display cases are often moved and small objects have been hurled at ghost investigators while footsteps and other unexplained sounds have been noted.

Both the *Discovery* and the *Unicorn* are open to the public.
For details of RRS *Discovery* telephone 01382 309060 or consult
<www.rrsdiscovery.com>
For HMS *Unicorn* telephone 01382 200900 or consult
<www.frigateunicorn.org>.

Fact or Fiction?

Finally, a short account of an experience of my own.

More years ago than I care to remember, a friend played the organ in one of the churches in Montrose.

One Saturday evening, the two of us had gone to the church so that she could run through a piece she was to play the following day. At one point, she went off to another room to fetch something, leaving me sitting alone in the front pew.

If you have ever sat in an empty church with the heating coming on you will know you can hear every creak and groan as the wood expands and contracts due to the temperature changing. The eerie effect that particular night was compounded by the fact that only the organ lights were on so that the bulk of the church was in semi darkness.

To the left of where I was sitting there was a door covered by a curtain to keep out the draught.

As I sat there, I heard the door open and then the curtain was drawn back, as if by unseen hands, followed by the sound of footsteps on the wooden floor. I could see no one.

Without a shadow of a doubt I was petrified. My brain told me to run while my legs, having turned to jelly, were unwilling to allow flight.

As I sat there wondering what I was witnessing, the Beadle's (Church Officer) daughter, aged around three or four and too small to be seen because of the pews at that side of the building, came into view.

So my 'ghost' experience had a logical explanation but had I been able to escape I would now be recounting it as a genuine ghost story.

There are further tales however lacking such simple explanations, often just an excerpt from someone's personal experience, as to why a particular incident or sequence of events occurred.

For example, there is the toddler, too young to know about ghosts, who continually asked her grandmother about the other baby in the house, although there was none.

There is the professional photographer who finished off a film in a customer's camera by taking the last few exposures in his shop. On developing the film he found an unexplained figure in the photographs he had taken. He could find no logical explanation for the 'extra member of staff' and his attempts to recreate the same scene failed to produce a similar result.

Some of these tales recalled here are obviously folk tales, the stuff of legend, while others were told to me by people whose judgement I respected, people who did not strike me as being in any way deluded or fanciful.

There are perhaps more things in heaven and earth than we know or understand. The question is, when it comes to ghosts and the supernatural – are you a believer or an atheist?

23 *A face? In fact the 'features' at the top of the picture are a trick of light. Picture courtesy of Alice & Neil McLeod.*

Bibliography

Aldridge, D. *The Rescue of Captain Scott* (East Linton: Tuckwell Press, 1999)

Breeze, D. *Roman Scotland Frontier Country* (London: B T Batsford, 2006)

Dennison & Coleman, *Historic Forfar; A Scottish Survey* (East Linton: Tuckwell Press, 2000)

Dingwall, E J. *The Minor Traditions of British Mythology* (1948)

Douglas, G. *Scottish Fairy & Folk Tales,* (1901)

Fraser, D. *Discovering Angus & Mearns* (Montrose: Standard Press, 1966)

Garvie, S. *Marriage To Murder* (Edinburgh: Chambers, 1980)

Harris, P. *The Garvie Trial* (Aberdeen: Impulse, 1969)

Jacob, V. *The Lairds of Dun* (London: John Murray, 1931)

Jervise, A. *Memorials of Angus & the Mearns* (Edinburgh, 1885)

Jervise, A. *The History & Traditions of the Lands of the Lindsays in Angus & the Mearns* (Edinburgh, 1853)

Keppie, L. *Scotland's Roman Remains* (Edinburgh: John Donald Publishers Ltd, 1990)

Lowson, A. *Tales, Legends and Traditions of Forfarshire* (Forfar: John Macdonald, 1891)

MacKinlay, J M. *Folklore of Scottish Lochs & Springs* (1893)

Montrose Air Station Museum Trust. *Montrose Airfield From 1913* (Montrose, 2000)

Montrose Basin Heritage Society, *Ebb & Flow,* (Balgavies, Angus: Pinkfoot Press, 2004)

Montrose Basin Heritage Society, *Flowing Past,* (Brechin: MBHS, 2008)

Ross, Blanche & Simpson, *The Greatest Squadron of Them All, Volume 1* (London: Grub Street, 2003)

Scharlau, F C. *The Story of the Forfar Witches* (Forfar: Angus District Council, 1995)

Williams, J. *The Modern Sherlock Holmes* (London: Broadside Books Ltd, 1991)

Other Sources

The Courier

Montrose Review

Montrose Air Station Heritage Centre Archives

Donaldson & Morpeth, *A Dictionary of Scottish History* (Edinburgh: John Donald Publishers, 1977)

Also by Forbes Inglis:

The Sea Enriches: A Gable Ender's trawl through time

210 mm; 144pp; b/w illustrations
ISBN 978 1 874012 61.0   PB   £8.99

From the time of William Wallace through to the emergence of North Sea Oil, the sea has been good to Montrose and its inhabitants, nicknamed the Gable Endies. *The Sea Enriches* reveals aspects of the history of the Royal Burgh following its progress from a small fishing/trading settlement to a prosperous burgh run by local merchants who were often ahead of their time regarding improvements to the town. The local newspaper, *The Montrose Review*, has been recording the story of Montrose since 1811 and, for almost 70 years, has run a feature by different writers under the byline 'Gable Ender'. Some of the current Gable Ender's columns, based on the *Review's* files and earlier sources, are gathered here to give a flavour of the town's past. Subjects include: the first lunatic asylum in Scotland; the first lifeboat in Scotland if not the UK; flirtation with renewable energy during the 1920s; the connection to the Tay Bridge disaster; piracy and the murder of a local crew in Brazil; and women's lib – 17th-century style – to a visit from the Iron Lady herself.

Murders & Misdeeds: Angus and Dundee 1765–1900

210 mm; 144pp; b/w illustrations
ISBN 978 1 874012 62 7   PB   £8.99

Fascinated by the story of Margaret Shuttleworth, the Montrose woman tried for the murder of her husband and convicted on the most circumstantial of evidence, Forbes Inglis embarked on a mission to discover more about the men and women who were accused of capital crimes in Angus and Dundee during the 18th and 19th centuries.

He uncovered many interesting stories, such as the trial of Kitty Nairn for incest and the murder of her husband, a man twenty years her senior, an accused who would have hung had the Crown been more careful in drawing up the indictment; the intriguing case of the Kirriemuir hotelier's wife who might, like other victims, have been responsible for her own death; and the enigma of the Dundee murderer William Bury – was he really Jack the Ripper?

Compounding the horror of the crimes themselves, until 1868 public hanging was the punishment meted out to most of those convicted of murder, which meant they paid the penalty in full view of a crowd gathered for the occasion so that justice could be seen to be done. Unfortunately, the hangmen of the time weren't always well prepared and there are tales of incompetence and at least one 'stand in' executioner.

In *Murders and Misdeeds* Forbes looks at the stories behind the trials and also speculates on how modern forensic science might have changed some of the verdicts.

More local publications from Pinkfoot Press

The History of Brechin, to 1864

David D Black

216mm; xii + 394pp; b/w illustrations
ISBN 978 1 874012 51 1   HB £14.99

A facsimile edition of David D Black's *History of Brechin* first published in 1839 with a revised and updated second edition in 1867. It is the latter edition which has been used here with some extra illustrations added by the publisher to a subsequent printing of 1900.

David Dakers Black was born in Brechin in 1797, the son of the city's Procurator-Fiscal. He also studied for the law and, on completion of his apprenticeship, went to Edinburgh for some time. He then returned to Brechin to practice as a writer (solicitor) and in 1825 he was appointed joint Town Clerk. The following year, on the death of the other incumbent, he became the sole officer, a position he held until his retirement in 1864. During his long tenure in the post, he apparently 'discharged his duties faithfully and well, keeping himself entirely free from the slightest suspicion of partisanship'. Also from 1836 until his death he managed a branch of the British Linen Company's Bank in Brechin. He made bequests to aid the education of boys and girls in the town and he actively worked for and supported many local charities.

However well respected he was in Brechin, Black was regarded somewhat differently in Shetland, where, having purchased the estate of Kergord, he subsequently cleared some 200 people from his land in Weisdale. It is said that he used stone from the evicted crofters' demolished cottages to build a substantial dwelling, the Haa of Flemington, which later became Kergord House, made famous in the Second World War as the base of the Shetland Bus, the covert operation assisting the Norwegian resistance movement. Black himself was proud of his acquisition in Shetland styling himself Black of Kergord, the name which appears on his memorial in Brechin cathedral cemetery.

Black's History of Brechin endures and, although somewhat dated now, it is still the first point of reference for anyone wishing to learn more about the ancient cathedral city.

The Pinkfoot Press
1 Pearse Street, Brechin, Angus, DD9 6JR

01356 626216
orders@pinkfootpress.co.uk

The Glens of Angus: Names, Places, People

David Dorward, with illustrations by Colin Gibson

210mm; viii + 160pp; 85 b/w illustrations; map
ISBN 978 1 874012 25 2   PB £7.99

A major place-name study of the hills and glens of Angus – a little-known but paradisiacal part of Scotland. Traversed by no through roads, but still readily accessible from the south, they have preserved their beauty and tranquillity to a quite unusual degree. It is not the aim of this book to change such a happy state of affairs, but rather to provide more information and greater insights to those who love quiet and unspoiled places.

The book covers many aspects of the area, from archaeology, history, wildlife, flora and land-ownership – mostly through the medium of the place-names, which long fascinated the author but had eluded comprehensive study.

The final section of the book comprises a gazetteer – more or less complete – of all the place-names of North Angus, with locations, derivations, pronunciations (and some diverting anecdotes). This is something which had not been attempted before.

The author spent most of his life within sight of the Angus hills and knew the area, on bike and foot, from boyhood. The book is copiously illustrated with drawings by the late Colin Gibson, the well-known and greatly beloved 'Nature Diarist' of the Courier.

David Dorward was born and educated in Dundee. A graduate of St Andrews University, he practised as a solicitor for a short time before joining the administrative staff of his old university where he remained for 32 years, eventually attaining the position of Secretary. David's other publications include: *Scottish Surnames*; *Scotland's Place-names*; *Dundee, Names, People and Places*; and, another Pinkfoot publication, *The Sidlaw Hills* (see over).

Dunnichen Hillfort: The building of a modern myth

David Henry

210 mm; 48pp; b/w illustrations
ISBN 978 1 874012 55 9   PB £4.99

The Battle of Nechtansmere or Duin Nechtain, was fought in AD685 between Northumbrian Angles and Picts under their respective kings Ecgfrith and Brude.

At the beginning of the 19th century, George Chalmers identified the site of this Pictish victory as Dunnichen in central Angus. Since then, historians of the battle have assumed that a prominent hillfort on Dunnichen Hill played an important role in the outcome of the Pictish victory.

This wide-ranging study attempts to reveal how this notion came about and why it has persisted despite the lack of tangible evidence for a fort on the hill.

The Sidlaw Hills

David Dorward, with illustrations by Colin Gibson

210mm; xiv + 162pp; 73 b/w illustrations
ISBN 978 1 874012 46 7   PB £7.99

Having already examined Dundee and the Angus glens in two highly successful books, David Dorward turned his attention to The Sidlaws, his beloved 'hills of home', which he had first explored as a boy growing up in Dundee. In this, his last book, which was completed just before his death in December 2003, but published posthumously, David explains something of his rekindled passion for his old stomping ground:

> One of the temptations to write about the Sidlaws is that they are relatively unknown, underused and greatly undervalued. I have lived for a fairish time and seen a bit of the world, at least in Europe, and some of the Americas, but it has taken me the best part of seventy years to come to the realisation that the Sidlaws are among the sweetest places on earth.

David treats his subject with a broad brush, but it is principally through his elucidation of the place-names that we are able to gain a better understanding of this wonderful, though unspectacular range of hills and of the history of the people who have inhabited the area, utilised its resources, and shaped the landscape.

As with David's previous publication, *The Glens of Angus*, this volume is profusely illustrated with drawings by Tayside's pre-eminent artist and naturalist, the late Colin Gibson.

The Battle of Dunnichen

Graeme Cruickshank

210mm; 52pp; 11 b/w illustrations
ISBN 978 1 874012 52 8   PB £4.99

A further edition of the acclaimed account of the Picts' famous victory over the Northumbrians at Dunnichen, or Nechtansmere, on 20 May 685.

Why did King Ecgfrith, a skilled and seasoned campaigner, ignore advice and lead his successful Northumbrian troops into Angus, the very heartland of Pictish territory, to do battle with the Picts and their king, Bruide? The battle resulted in humiliating defeat for the Northumbrians and Ecgfrith himself was slain and his army routed.

In this well-researched study, Graeme Cruickshank skilfully pieces together the surviving evidence to construct a convincing picture of the events surrounding the battle and of the chief protagonists, Bruide and Ecgfrith.

The decisive Pictish victory ensured freedom forever from Northumbrian control over not only southern Pictland, but of the territories of the Britons and Scots that they also held. Such is the importance of the battle that Cruickshank concludes that without it 'there may well never have been a Scottish nation'.

A Life on the Land: farming in Angus 1934–1994

Harry Brown
Edited by David Orr

210mm; 76pp; b/w illustrations, map
ISBN 978 1 874012 32 0   PB £4.99

Harry Brown's working life on the land began in 1934 and lasted until his retirement, 60 years later, in 1994. Initially fee'd to work at various farms around Forfar in central Angus, usually for a fixed term of six months, he progressed through the bothy system from 'loon' to 'first horseman', eventually ending up managing his own farm. During his time Harry witnessed many changes in agricultural practices and these are all documented in this fascinating account. Most intriguing are his memories of working with horses, the feeing markets and bothy life, and he also shares glimpses of some of the many characters he worked alongside.

Possessing an uncanny ability to clearly recall people and events from his past, Harry, astonishingly, remembers the names and positions of all the people whom he came into contact with through his work. It is even more surprising to learn that not a word of his reminiscences had been written down until he related them to David Orr.

Anyone interested in the land and history of Angus will appreciate the authentic voice of the author in this welcome addition to the agricultural and social history of 20th-century Scotland – subjects more usually the preserve of specialist writers and academic researchers.

The Parish of Dunnichen 1791 & 1833: The 'First' and 'New' Statistical Accounts

Edited by David Henry

210mm; 28pp; illuss
ISBN 978 1 874012 57 3   PB £3.99

Two men, George Dempster of Dunnichen and Rev James Headrick were closely associated with Sir John Sinclair, the supervisor and editor of the 'First' *Statistical Account of Scotland* published in 21 volumes from 1791 to 1799. They were all concerned with transforming the state of the country through agriculture, fisheries, and manufacturing, thereby increasing the wealth of the nation and improving the social conditions of a growing population, and viewed the Statistical Account as a means of promoting reform. Dempster supplied the report on Dunnichen parish for the 1791 volume and Headrick wrote the 'new' report in 1833, although it was not published until 1845, and thus put the small parish of Dunnichen, in the heart of rural Angus, at the forefront of improvement and development in Scotland during the period of the agricultural and industrial revolutions.

The Pinkfoot Press, 1 Pearse Street, Brechin, Angus DD9 6JR